GAZA
STAY HUMAN

GAZA
STAY HUMAN

Vittorio Arrigoni

With a preface by
Ilan Pappé

Translated by
Daniela Filippin

KUBE
PUBLISHING

First published in England by
Kube Publishing Ltd.,
Markfield Conference Centre
Ratby Lane, Markfield,
Leicestershire LE67 9SY
United Kingdom
Tel: +44 (0) 1530 249230
Fax: +44 (0) 1530 249656
Website: www.kubepublishing.com
Email: info@kubepublishing.com

Originally published as *Gaza: Restiamo Umani*,
Il Manifesto – Manifestolibri, 2009.

Cataloguing-in-Publication Details are available from the British Library

ISBN 978-1-84774-019-9 *paperback*

With thanks to
Mohammed Al-Zaanoun (Mohammedzaanoun@yahoo.com)
and Majdi Fathi (Majdi_pal@hotmail.com) for providing
the cover image and other photos for the book.

Typesetting: NA Qaddoura
Cover design: Nasir Cadir

Printed by: Imak Ofset - Turkey

Contents

Source: Wikimedia, Creative Commons Licence 3.0, Gringer, 2009

Preface: The Killing Fields of Gaza, 2009

In 2004, the Israeli army began building a dummy Arab city in the Negev Desert. It's the size of a real city, with streets – all of them given names – mosques, public buildings and cars. Built at a cost of $45 million, this phantom city became a dummy Gaza in the winter of 2006, after Hizbullah fought Israel to a draw in the north, so that the Israeli Defence Force (IDF) could prepare to fight a 'better war' against Hamas in the south.

When the Israeli Chief of General Staff Dan Halutz visited the site after the Lebanon war, he told the press that soldiers 'were preparing for the scenario that will unfold in the dense neighbourhood of Gaza City'. A week into the bombardment of Gaza, Ehud Barak attended a rehearsal for the ground war. Foreign television crews filmed him as he watched ground troops conquer the dummy city, storming the empty houses and no doubt killing the 'terrorists' hiding in them.

In 2005, Gaza became a military target in the official Israeli view, as if it were a huge enemy base and not a place of civilian and human habitation. Gaza should not be treated differently from Barcelona, Brighton, Lyon or any other city in the world but for the Israelis it became a dummy city for soldiers to experiment with the most advanced weapons.

It all began after Israel 'disengaged' from Gaza in the summer of 2005. The settlers were moved so as to enable the Israel army to control the Strip and employ harsh, retaliatory and punitive action without worrying about the fate of Jewish settlers in it. It was hoped that this cynical act would look like a peace gesture, which indeed it did – for a while at least.

But things did not turn out the way they were expected to. The eviction was followed by a Hamas takeover, first in democratic elections, then in a pre-emptive coup staged to avert an American-backed seizure by Fatah. The immediate Israeli response was to impose an economic blockade on the Strip. Hamas retaliated by firing missiles at Sderot, giving Israel a pretext to use its air force, artillery and gunships. Israel claimed to be shooting at 'the launching areas of the missiles', but in practice this meant anywhere and everywhere in Gaza.

Tank shelling, bombing from the air and the sea, and brutal incursions were a frequent sight. But when Israel was defeated on another front, that of Southern Lebanon in the summer of 2006, the army escalated its punitive action against 1.5 million people living in the densest 40 square kilometres on the globe. The policy became more and more genocidal and the Hamas reaction to it more desperate. The escalation was caused by the humiliation of the Israeli army in Lebanon by the Hizbullah. The army needed to show its superiority and deterrence capability deemed by it to be the main safeguards for the Jewish state's survival in a 'hostile' world. The Islamic nature of both the Hamas and the Hizbullah and an alleged, and totally faked, association of both with al-Qaeda, enabled the army to imagine an Israel spearheading a global war against jihadism in Gaza.

While George W. Bush was in power, the killing of women and babies in Gaza could be accepted even by the American administration as being part of that holy war against Islam.

The genodical policy began in earnest in the first month of 2007 and has reached its horrible crescendo in January 2009. Already in 2007 the casualties were high: 300 people were killed in Gaza, dozens of them children.

But even under Bush, and definitely in the post-Bush era, the myth of fighting global jihad in Gaza was losing the IDF credibility. So a new mythology was proposed in 2007: Gaza was a terrorist base determined to destroy Israel. The only way the Palestinian could be 'de-terrorised', so to speak, was to consent to live in a Strip encircled by barbed wire and walls. Supply, as well as movement in and out of the Strip, depended on the political choice made by the Gazans. Should they persist in supporting the Hamas, they would be strangulated and starved until they changed their ideological inclination. Should they succumb to the kind of politics Israel wishes them to adopt, they would suffer the same fate as that of the West Bank: life without basic civil and human rights. They could either be inmates of the open prison of the West Bank or the maximum security one in the Gaza Strip. If they resist they are likely to be imprisoned without trial, or killed. This is Israel's message.

The people of Gaza were given a year, 2008, to make up their mind. They opted for resistance and the reaction was the January 2009 massacre. The dummy city became the real Gaza and it was brutally attacked with the might reserved by conventional armies to face tank brigades and infantry division in an open battlefield, not in a human rural and urban space. Gaza also became the killing fields for the most updated forms of weaponry, the usage of which is strictly forbidden by the international community and is regarded as a war crime.

Resistance in Palestine has always been based in villages and towns: where else could it come from? That is why Palestinian cities, towns and villages, dummy or real, have been depicted ever since the 1936 Arab revolt as 'enemy bases' in military plans and orders. Any retaliation or punitive action is bound to target civilians, among whom there may be a handful of people who are involved in active resistance against Israel. Haifa was treated as an enemy base in 1948, as was Jenin in 2002; now Beit Hanoun, Rafah and Gaza are regarded that way. When you have the firepower, and no moral inhibitions against massacring civilians, you get the situation we are now witnessing in Gaza.

But it is not only in military discourse that Palestinians are dehumanised. A similar process is at work in Jewish civil society in Israel, and it explains the massive support there for the carnage in Gaza. Palestinians have been so dehumanised by Israeli Jews – whether politicians, soldiers or ordinary citizens – that killing them comes naturally, as did expelling them in 1948, or imprisoning them in the Occupied Territories. The current Western response indicates that its political leaders fail to see the direct connection between the Zionist dehumanisation of the Palestinians and Israel's barbarous policies in Gaza. There is a grave danger that the sequel to 'Operation Cast Lead' would turn Gaza into a ghost town similar to the dummy village built in the Negev.

Indeed, in order to appreciate the shocking document you are about to read, you have to realise how indifferent it would leave the vast majority of the Israeli Jews, should they be willing to read and engage with this crucially important book. One of the great attributes of this book is that it is and first and foremost an eyewitness account of an everyman and a true humanist. And who knows that this account might open up a small window for closed minds that support Israel unconditionally.

I came back to Israel after a long while when the January 2009 genocidal Israeli attack on Gaza commenced. The state, through its media and with the help of its academia, broadcasted with one unanimous voice – even louder than the one heard during the criminal attack against Lebanon in the summer of 2006. Israel was engulfed once more with righteous fury that translates into destructive policies in the Gaza Strip. This appalling self-justification for inhumanity and impunity was not just annoying; it is a subject worth dwelling on, if one wants to understand the international indefference to the massacre that rages on in Gaza.

It is based first and foremost on sheer lies transmitted with a newspeak reminiscent of darker days in 1930s Europe. During the onslaught on Gaza, every half-an-hour a news bulletin on the radio and television described the victims of Gaza as terrorists and Israel's massive killings of them as an act of self-defence. Israel presented itself to its own people as a righteous victim defending itself against a great evil. The academic world was recruited to explain how demonic and monstrous the Palestinian struggle was, as it was led by Hamas. These were the same scholars who demonized the late Palestinian leader Yasser Arafat in an earlier era and delegitimized his Fatah movement during the second Palestinian Intifada.

But the lies and distorted representations were not the worst part of it. It was the direct attack on the last vestiges of humanity and dignity of the Palestinian people that was most enraging. The Palestinians in Israel have shown their solidarity with the people of Gaza and were consequently branded as a fifth column in the Jewish state; their right to remain in their homeland cast as doubtful given their lack of support for the Israeli aggression. Those among them who agreed – wrongly, in my opinion – to appear in the local media were interrogated, and not interviewed, as if they were inmates in the Shin Bet's prison. Their appearance was prefaced and followed by humiliating racist remarks and they were met with accusations of being an irrational and fanatical people. And yet this was not the basest practice. There were a few Palestinian children from the occupied territories treated for cancer in Israeli hospitals. God knows what price their families paid for them to be admitted there. Israel Radio went to the hospital daily to demand from the poor parents that they tell the Israeli audience how right Israel was to attack and how evil Hamas was in its defence.

There were no boundaries to the hypocrisy that a righteous fury produces. The discourse of the generals and the politicians moved erratically between complimenting the army for the humanity it displays in its 'surgical' operations on the one hand, and the need to destroy Gaza for once and for all on the other, in a humane way of course.

This righteous fury is a constant feature in the Israeli, and before that Zionist, dispossession of Palestine. Every act – whether it was ethnic cleansing, occupation, massacre or destruction – was always portrayed as morally just and as a pure act of self-defence, reluctantly perpetrated by Israel in its war against the worst kind of human beings. From Left to Right, from Likud to Kadima, from the academia to the media, one can hear this righteous fury of a state that is busier than any other state in the world in destroying and dispossessing an indigenous population.

It is crucial to explore the ideological origins of this attitude and derive the necessary political conclusions from its prevalence. This righteous fury shields the society and politicians in Israel from any external rebuke or criticism. But far worse, it is always translated into destructive policies against the Palestinians documented so chillingly, and yet so humanly, in this book.

The author Vittorio Arrigoni volunteered with the International Solidarity Movement to help the people of Gaza as part of its mission to protect human rights. He was there during and after Operation 'Cast Lead' and so his daily dispatches came directly from the killing fields of Gaza, and are therefore free of any media distortion or manipulation.

It is through this account that we can see how in the eyes of average Israeli Jews, bereft of any effective internal criticism or external pressure, every Palestinian becomes a potential target of this fury. Given the firepower of the Jewish state it can inevitably only end in more massive killings, massacres and ethnic cleansing. Much of what you will read in this book is about the heroic attempt of volunteers such as Vittorio Arrigoni to shield the people of Gaza from this ferocious aggression. But it will not prove to be enough to save the Palestinians.

The righteous fury of many Israelis is a powerful act of self-denial and justification. It explains why Israeli Jewish society may not be moved by words of wisdom, logical persuasion or diplomatic dialogue. And if one does not want to endorse violence as the means of opposing it, there is only one way forward: challenging head-on this righteousness as an evil ideology meant to cover human atrocities. Another name for this ideology is Zionism and an international rebuke for Zionism, not just for particular Israeli policies, is the only way of countering this self-righteousness. We have to try and explain not only to the world, but also to the Israelis themselves, that Zionism is an ideology that endorses ethnic cleansing, occupation and now massive massacres. What is needed now is not just a condemnation of the present massacre but also de-legitimization of the ideology that produced that policy and justifies it morally and politically. Let us hope that significant voices in the world will tell the Jewish state that this ideology and the overall conduct of the state are intolerable and unacceptable and as long as they persist, Israel will be boycotted and subject to sanctions.

Almost a year after the massacre, alas, these hopes are not yet vindicated. Even the killing of hundreds of innocent Palestinians was not enough to produce any significant shift in the Western public opinion, let alone in the position of the Western governments. It seems that even the most horrendous crimes, such as the genocide in Gaza, are treated as discrete events, unconnected to anything that happened in the past and are not associated with any ideology or system.

August 2009   **Ilan Pappé**

For the reader: a warning and instructions for use

'Stay human' is the motto with which I sign off my pieces for *Il Manifesto* and for the entries on my blog. It's an invitation, or, better still, a prompt, to desist from the commission of criminal acts and to reaffirm and take possession of the original purposes of humankind instead. Once boundaries, flags, barriers, latitudes and ethno-religious differences have been abolished, what breaks onto the scene of life is a scenario stripped of the impulse to preserve one's own kin at the expense of others. Mine is an invitation to remember our belonging to a sole community of living beings: the human family.

Gaza: Stay Human is now also a book. Please find within the three-week story of a massacre, written to the best of my ability, more often than not in very precarious conditions, often scribbling about the inferno all around me in a tattered notebook while crouched in an ambulance screaming down the street. Or frantically tapping away at the keyboard of any available computer I could find, often inside a building shaking like a crazed pendulum as explosions went off all around. I must warn you that leafing through this book could prove dangerous. These are harmful pages, blood-stained, imbued with white phosphorous, and as sharp as bomb shrapnel. If read within the quiet of a bedroom, your walls will shake from our cries of terror. I feel concerned for the walls of your hearts, which I recognize have not yet become soundproofed to pain.

Please store this volume somewhere safe, within the reach of the young, so that they may immediately learn of a world not so far away from them, where indifference and racism tears their peers to little bits as if they were mere rag dolls. This way they may be inoculated against racism from an early age, against any epidemic of violence towards whoever is different, or against neutrality when faced with injustice. *Gaza: Stay Human* aims to float beyond other books written about, in and around Palestine thanks to the creative fire that has begotten it: the keen will of this author to involve, enlighten and heighten the reader's awareness of what atrocious inhumanities unfolded during those 22 days of a massacre. This is my small contribution towards preventing similar massacres from ever taking place in future. Giving the dead some justice and safeguarding tomorrow's mortally wounded.

Please help yourself to a ticket for a tour of hell that even the poet Dante Alighieri could not have conceived of when waking up from his pillow, full of nightmares. I entertain the hope of having been a good guide throughout to this hell, like Dante's Charon, the ferryman of Hades, of having been as faithful and as humane as possible in my narration. Standing in the rubble of a freshly-bombed building or in the ward of a Gaza hospital, I'm aware that it was sometimes difficult to recognize human features in what was once a face, now mutated, reduced to a pulp by devastating weaponry that is mostly banned by all international conventions. My account strives for the greatest possible objectivity. As it happens, I was myself an object, or target, of the Israeli army and also received death threats from a group of neo-Nazis connected with some settler groups. For whomsoever is still in doubt, months after the massacre, my account and the details recorded underneath a storm of bombs have been backed up by all the most reliable human rights organizations, whether governmental or otherwise, as well as by Israeli soldiers themselves, who have recently started to confess the crimes they have committed. In time, *Gaza: Stay Human* will become increasingly more like an historic document rather than being a plain narrative from hell.

If truth is the first victim of war, it is then Israel's absolute priority to assassinate it, before, during and after the conflict. Our duty as activists, and more generally as human beings, is to document and tell the truth for the sake of freedom and justice, and then bring it to the table of world public opinion, and then serve it as a meal, the more difficult to digest the better.

For tomorrow, so as to stay human.

The port (or its rubble),   **Vittorio Arrigoni**
Gaza City
15th July 2009

My apartment in Gaza faces the sea, a panoramic view that's always done wonders for my mood, often challenged by all the misery that a life under siege can bring. That is, before this morning, when all hell broke loose outside my window. We woke up to the sound of bombs dropping, many of them falling a few hundred metres from my home. Some of my friends have fallen under them.

So far the death toll has reached 210, but it's bound to rise dramatically. It's an unprecedented bloodshed. They've razed the port facing my apartment to the ground, and pulverized police stations. I've been told that the Western media are on-message and are repeating the press releases issued by the Israeli military parrot-style, according to which the attacks only targeted Hamas's terrorist dens with surgical precision.

In actual fact, when visiting Al-Shifa, the city's main hospital, and gazing over chaotic lines of bodies laid out in its courtyard, we mostly saw civilians among those awaiting treatment, lying randomly alongside other bodies, awaiting rightful burial.

Can you picture Gaza? Every house leans against another, every building rises over the next one. Gaza is the

1

place with the highest population density in the world, which means that when you bomb from a height of 10,000 metres, you'll inevitably butcher many civilians. You're aware of it, you're guilty as charged, it's no error, and certainly no case of collateral damage either. When shelling the central police station in Al-Abbas, the neighbouring elementary school was also damaged by the explosion. It was the end of the school day and the children were already in the street. Most of their flapping sky-blue aprons were splashed with blood.

When bombing the Dair Al-Balah police academy, some dead and wounded were also recorded from the souk nearby, this being Gaza's central market. We've seen the bodies of animals and humans mixing their blood in rivulets trickling down the asphalt roads. A Guernica transfigured into reality.

I saw many corpses in uniforms in the various hospitals I visited – I knew many of those boys. I greeted them every day when I met them in the street on my way to the port, or walked to the central café of an evening. I knew several of them by name. A name, a history, a mutilated family.

The majority were young, around 18 or 20, mostly without political leanings, neither siding with Fatah nor Hamas, simply enrolled into the police force once they had finished university in order to have a secure job in Gaza, which under Israel's criminal siege has more than 60% unemployment among its population. I have no interest in propaganda and let my eyes bear witness, my ears stay in tune with the screaming sirens and the rumbling of TNT.

I haven't seen any terrorists among the casualties today, only civilians and policemen. Just last night I poked fun at

28th December 2008: A Palestinian family on the run after an Israeli missile hit the refugee camp in Rafah (AP/Eyad Baba)

a couple of them for the way they were cloaked up against the cold, as they stood in front of my house.

I want the truth to redeem these dead.

They'd never fired a single shot against Israel, nor would they have ever done so – it wasn't in their job description to do so. They acted as traffic wardens, took care of internal security. The port is quite a distance from the Israeli border anyway.

I own a video camera, but today I discovered what a terrible cameraman I am. I can't bring myself to film mangled bodies or faces drenched in tears. I just can't. I start crying myself.

The other International Solidarity Movement (ISM) volunteers and I went to Al-Shifa Hospital to give blood.

That's where we received a call informing us that Sara, a dear friend, had been killed by a piece of shrapnel near her home in the refugee camp of Jabalia. She was a sweet person, a sunny soul, and had gone out to buy some bread for her family. She leaves 13 children behind.

A moment ago I got a call from Tawfiq, from Cyprus. Tawfiq is one of the Palestinian students lucky enough to have left the enormous prison camp of Gaza on one of our Free Gaza Movement boats, to start anew somewhere else. He asked me if I'd visited his uncle and whether I had gone to say hello on his behalf, as I had promised. Hesitatingly, I apologized because I hadn't found the time. And it was too late anyway – he was buried by the rubble in the port area along with many others.

Israel launches the terrible threat that this is just the first day of a bombing campaign that could last for up to two weeks. They want to make a desert and then call it peace. The 'civilized' world's silence is more deafening than the explosions covering the city like a shroud of death and terror.

Stay human.

Subject: Dying slowly while listening out in vain

Date: 29th December 2008

From: Vittorio Arrigoni

An acrid smell of sulphur fills the air while the sky is shaken by earth-shattering rumbles. My ears are now deaf to the explosions and my eyes are all out of tears from all the corpses. I stand in front of Al-Shifa, Gaza's main hospital, when we receive Israel's latest, terrible threat: they intend to bomb the wing that is under construction. This wouldn't be a first, as Wea'm Hospital was bombed just yesterday, along with a medicine warehouse in Rafah, the Islamic university, and various mosques scattered along the Strip. Not to mention many other civilian infrastructures. Apparently, no longer able to find 'sensible' targets, the air force and navy now are killing time targeting places of worship, schools and hospitals.

It's another 9/11 every single hour, every minute around here, and tomorrow is always a new day for mourning, bringing equal desperation. You notice the helicopters and airplanes constantly overhead, you see a flash, but you're already a goner and it's too late to take flight. There are no bunkers against the bombs in the Strip and no place is really safe. I can't contact my friends in Rafah, not even those who live north of Gaza City, hopefully because the phone lines are overloaded. Hopefully. I haven't slept in 60 hours, and the same can be said of any Gazan.

Yesterday three other ISM members and I spent the night at the Al-Awda Hospital in the Jabalia refugee camp. We were there in fearful expectation of the much-dreaded ground raid that never happened. But the Israeli tanks are strung all along the Strip's borders as we speak, creaking their way into a funeral procession. Around 11.30pm, a bomb fell about 800 metres from the hospital, the shock wave blowing several windows apart and injuring the injured. An ambulance rushed to the spot where a mosque had been shelled, but it was thankfully empty at the time. Unfortunately (though it actually has nothing to do with fortune, rather with the deliberate criminal and terrorising will to massacre civilians), the Israeli bomb had also struck the building adjacent to the mosque, which was likewise destroyed.

We watched as the tiny bodies of six little sisters were pulled out of the rubble – five are dead, one is in a life-threatening condition. They laid the little girls out onto the blackened asphalt, and they looked like broken dolls, disposed of as they were no longer usable. This wasn't a mistake, but a wilful and cynical horror.

We're now at a toll of 320 dead, more than a thousand wounded and, according to a doctor at Al-Shifa, 60% of those are destined to die in the next few hours or days, after enduring a prolonged agony.

There are many missing. For the last two days despairing wives have been searching for their husbands or children in the hospitals, often to no avail. The morgue is a macabre spectacle. A nurse told me that, after hours of searching through body parts in the refrigerator cell, a Palestinian woman recognized her husband's amputated hand. That was all that was left of her husband, along with the wedding band on her finger, a remnant of the eternal love they had sworn to one another. Out of a house once inhabited by two families, very little remained of their bodies. They showed their relatives half of one torso and three legs.

Right now, one of our Free Gaza Movement boats is leaving the port in Larnaca, Cyprus. I spoke to my friends on board. They've heroically amassed medicine and packed it tightly onto the boat. It should reach the port of Gaza tomorrow around 8.00pm. Here's to hoping that the port will still exist after another night of non-stop shelling. I'll be in touch with them during the entire night.

Please, someone stop this nightmare.

Choosing to remain silent means somehow lends support to the genocide unfolding right now. Shout out your indignation, in every capital of the 'civilised' world, in every city, in every square, covering our own screams of pain and terror.

A slice of humanity is dying while pitifully listening out for a response.

Stay human.

29th December 2008: A mourner holds the body of a
four-year-old, one of five members of a family killed by an
Israeli missile (AP/Hatem Moussa)

Subject: The Angel Factories

Date: 30th December 2008

From: Vittorio Arrigoni

Jabilia, Beit Hanoun, Rafah, and Gaza City are the legs of the journey in my personal map of hell. Whatever the press releases from the Israeli military leadership may say, recited parrot-style all over Europe and the US via the disinformation experts, in the last few days I've been an eyewitness to the bombing of mosques, schools, universities, hospitals, markets and many, many civilian buildings.

The medical director at Al-Shifa Hospital has confirmed he received calls from members of the IDF, the Israeli Army, ordering him to evacuate the hospital, or else face being showered by missiles. But they never let the Army intimidate them. I should be sleeping at the port (although we haven't shut our eyes once in Gaza for at least four days), which is being constantly bombed at night. You no longer hear the sirens of ambulances in a mad chase, simply because there isn't a living soul left at the port or its environs. Everyone is dead, and it feels like treading through a cemetery in the aftermath of an earthquake.

The situation is really that of an unnatural catastrophe, a hate-fuelled and cynical upheaval catapulted onto the people of Gaza like molten lead, tearing human bodies

9

apart. Contrarily to all predictions, it unites all Palestinians, brought together by their collective endurance of a horrific massacre. These are people who may not even have greeted one another until recently, on account of belonging to opposing factions. But when the bombs shower down from the sky from a height of 10,000 metres, you can be sure they won't make a distinction between a Hamas or Fatah banner hanging from your window. They're no less explosive, even when you're Italian. There's no such thing as a surgically precise military operation. When the Air Force and the Navy start bombing, the only surgical operations are those tackled by the doctors, unhesitatingly amputating limbs reduced to a pulp, even when those arms and legs might have been spared. There's no time, you have to run, and the time you use to treat a seriously injured limb may spell death for the next wounded patient in line awaiting a transfusion, or worse. At Al-Shifa Hospital, 600 inpatients are in very serious condition, with only 29 ventilators available. They're short of everything, especially experienced staff.

For this precise reason, exhausted as we were (not so much by the sleepless nights as by the apathy and compliance of Western governments with Israel's crimes), we decided that last night was time for one of our Free Gaza Movement boats to leave the port of Larnaca, Cyprus, ferrying over medical staff and three tonnes of medicine. I waited for them in vain – they ought to have docked at 8am this morning. Instead, they were intercepted by 11 Israeli war ships at 90 nautical miles from Gaza, trying to sink them in full international waters. They rammed into them three times, provoking an engine failure and a leak in the hull. By pure chance the crew and passengers are all still alive, and have managed to dock the boat at the port of Tiro, in southern Lebanon.

Feeling increasingly frustrated by the 'civilized' world's deafening silence, my companions will make a second attempt soon. They've in fact unloaded the medicine from our damaged boat, the *Dignity*, and filled another boat ready for departure, heading straight for Gaza.

Many journalists who interview me ask me about the humanitarian situation of Palestinians in Gaza, as if the problem amounted just to food, water, electricity and fuel shortages, rather than the matter being about who is actually causing all of this by closing the borders, and bombing the water plant or electric power stations.

At the Al-Awda Hospital in Jabalia I've seen corpses and wounded bodies flooding in not only in ambulances, but on animal-drawn wooden carts. Tanks, fighter planes, drones, Apache helicopters – the world's fiercest army attacking a people who use donkeys as their main means of transportation, like in Jesus Christ's time. According to Al-Mezan, a human rights monitoring centre, while we speak 55 children have been killed in bombings, 20 are dying and 40 are seriously injured.

Israel has turned the Palestinian hospitals and morgues into angel factories, not realizing just how much hatred they are generating in Palestine and the rest of the world. The angel factories are churning out angels at the rate of a non-stop production line tonight as well: I can tell from the rumbles of explosions outside my window.

Those tiny dismembered and amputated bodies, those lives snuffed out before they had a chance to blossom, will be a recurrent nightmare for the rest of my life. If I can still find the strength to talk about this, it's only because I want to bring justice to those who no longer have a voice, those who've never had a hint of a voice, perhaps for the benefit of those who've never had ears.

Stay human.

Subject: The Unnatural Catastrophe

Date: 1st January 2009

From: Vittorio Arrigoni

The New Year just came in with the same omens of bleakness and death as the old one, increasing its destructive power tenfold. I've never seen so many bombs drop all around my apartment in front of the port. An explosion just 100 metres away violently shook our seven-storey building, making it rock like a crazed pendulum. For an instant, while the window panes exploded, we dreaded it would topple over. It was a major moment of panic in which I prayed and clung to the unlikely illusion that our building had been built using earthquake-proof criteria, even though Gaza is perched upon a strip of land that never quakes. Around here earthquakes are of the unnatural kind, and they're called Israel.

I continue with my desperate search for those friends who no longer pick up their phone. I heard from Ahmed at his place, one of the few houses still standing in the centre of the Tal El-Hawa neighbourhood in Gaza City, now surrounded by a post-apocalyptic scenario so reminiscent of the Shiite neighbourhood in Beirut after the bombs razed it to the ground in 2006, those bombs having been produced in the same part of the world as those falling on our heads right now. Ahmed is OK and so are his relatives, though his mother had a brush with death last Saturday. She teaches at the United Nations' Balqees School. On that day she'd stayed on in the classroom for a little longer than usual, which ended up saving her life. Many of her students, standing at the bus stop, were buried by the rubble produced after an explosion.

A bomb fell onto Ahmed's car, a pistachio-green economy car, the very same with which he roamed the city the previous evening, in search of some bread in a city where flour is being sold at the price of gold. As for Rafiq, in the end I reached him on the phone. His cavernous voice seemed to rise up from a deep well, a pit of desperation and sadness, from having just heard of the death of three best friends during the attack on the port.

In one of the last cafés still operating in Gaza, providing caffeine and an internet connection, smiling wryly, I showed a couple of friends a news article on my laptop speaking of 'one victim and 382 wounded'. This wasn't an estimate of the victims provoked by the Qassam 'rockets' shot against Israel yesterday, thankfully harming no one, but the aftermath of the 'massacre' our New Year's Eve firework displays had provoked in Italy. I told my friends that Hamas are wet behind the ears if they think they can compete with Israel using those homemade toys of theirs. They ought to take lessons in Naples to produce truly lethal rockets. As a pacifist and non-violent person, I abhor any form of Palestinian attack against Israel, but out here we're sick to the back teeth of hearing that tired old adage that this massacre of civilians was Israel's answer to the Palestinians launching their modest, homemade 'rockets'. For precision's sake, from 2002 to the present-day the Qassam

14

rockets against Israel have produced 18 dead, while only last Saturday, in just a couple of hours, we counted more than 250 civilian casualties in the hospitals.

At the café I enquire about the ceasefire proposed by the European Union and rejected by Israel, clearly still in possession of the vast supplies of war equipment it needs to use up from its arsenals. They all shake their heads grimly. Had there ever really been a truce before this fierce attack upon an unarmed population commenced? In November alone, the Israeli Army killed a good 17 Palestinians (43 in total from the start of the 'ceasefire'). And even before that, the criminal siege of Gaza had produced more than 200 dead among the Palestinian sick. The sick, with their papers in order, and waiting to find treatment in foreign hospitals, were prevented from getting anywhere with the borders being sealed off. The criminal siege of Israel has destroyed an already shaky economy, producing a rate of more than 60% unemployed, forcing 80% of Palestinian families to live off humanitarian aid. This is aid trickling through with huge difficulty, crossing the iron curtain erected by Israel around the largest open-air prison in the world: Gaza.

We were soon forced to evacuate that café, and fast. The umpteenth threatening phone call had come in: the café would be bombed within a few minutes. The crimes against humanity that Israel is soiling its hands with in these hours know few limits or terms of comparison. Yesterday at the Jabilia refugee camp an F16 plane dropped some missiles onto an ambulance. A doctor, Ihab El-Madhoun, and his trusted nurse, Mohamed Abu Hasira, both died. For this reason, today, we ISM volunteers have appeared at a press conference before the cameras of the most popular Palestinian television stations. We informed Israel that we'll hop on to those ambulances, hoping that our presence as internationals may act as a slight deterrent against these inhumane and bloody crimes.

Sometimes, our conversations get pretty bleak: it's likely that at the end of this massive, blood-curdling attack, some of us will have to go out there and do a final count of the dramatic toll of the dead and missing. We try not to think about it for now.

Stay human.

Subject: Ghosts demanding Justice

Date: 3rd January 2009

From: Vittorio Arrigoni

As I type this, Israeli tanks have entered the Strip. The day has begun the same way as the previous one ended, with the earth shaking beneath our feet, the sky and sea conniving endlessly against us overhead, hanging over the destinies of a million-and-a-half people who've gone from the tragedy of living under siege to the catastrophe of a targeted attack on civilians. The horizon is devastated by the flames, and there've been cannon shots rumbling from the sea and bombs raining from the sky all morning.

The same fishing boats we accompanied into the open sea just a few days ago, well beyond the six miles imposed by Israel in their illegal and criminal siege, are now reduced to charred wrecks. If the firefighters tried to put out the fires, they'd instantly become the targets of the F16's machine guns – this already happened yesterday.

After yet another attack, once the exact estimate of the dead is out (if this will ever be possible), the city will have to be rebuilt over a desert of rubble. Israel's Foreign Minister, Tzipi Livni, is declaring to the world that 'there is no humanitarian emergency in Gaza'. Clearly, 'being in denial' isn't the sole preserve of figures like Mahmoud Ahmadinejad, the Iranian president. The Palestinians are in agreement on one thing with Tzipi Livni (as Joseph, an ambulance driver, who calls her 'an ex-serial killer from the Mossad', tells me): more food is indeed coming in through the borders, simply because in December, next to nothing had managed to make it across the barbed wire fence put up by Israel. But what point is there in serving freshly baked bread in a cemetery?

The first priority ought to be stopping the bombing immediately, well before bringing any supplies to the survivors. Corpses don't eat: they can only provide compost for the earth, and, at the moment, Gaza has never been more fertile from decomposition. On the other hand, the disembowelled bodies of the children in the morgues ought to increase the sense of guilt in the indifferent lookers-on, those who *could have* done something. The images of a smiling Barack Obama, the US President, playing golf were shown on all the Arabic satellite TV stations, as if to scorn the shroud of mourning covering this land (and, as it happens, out here no one is under any illusion that Obama will do wonders to change America's foreign policy radically).

Yesterday, Israel opened the Erez Pass to evacuate all foreigners who are still currently in Gaza. We internationals of the ISM are the only ones to have remained. Today we addressed the Israeli government by means of a press conference, explaining the motives that commit us to staying put. We're disgusted by the passes being opened for the evacuation of foreigners, the only possible eyewitnesses to this massacre, while they are being kept well shut to the flow of international doctors and nurses pressing to get in and bring their heroic Palestinian colleagues some relief.

We're not going anywhere because we believe that our presence is essential to provide eyewitness accounts of the crimes inflicted against an unarmed civilian population hour-by-hour, minute-by-minute. We're now up to 445 dead, with over 2,300 wounded and many, many more missing. As I write this, 63 minors have been torn apart by bombs. At the moment Israel has counted three victims in total. We haven't fled, as our consulates have advised us to do, because we're well aware that our contribution as human shields on the ambulances in giving first aid could be decisive in saving lives. Once again, yesterday, an ambulance was hit in Gaza City. On the previous day two doctors at the Jabalia refugee camp had died when they were hit by a missile shot from an Apache helicopter. Personally, I'm not leaving the Strip because my friends have implored me not to abandon them, my surviving friends, as well as the dead ones, who crowd my sleepless nights like ghosts. Their diaphanous faces are still smiling at me.

7.33pm, Red Crescent Hospital in Jabalia. While I was connected via phone to the demonstrating crowds in Milan, two bombs fell in front of the hospital. The front windows were shattered, and, by pure chance, the ambulances were not damaged. The shelling has become more frequent and powerful in the last few hours. Nearby, Ibrahim Maqadme Mosque has just crumbled under the bombs: it's the tenth in a week. Eleven victims for now, and about 50 wounded. An elderly Palestinian lady I met in the street this afternoon asked me whether Israel thought it was still in the Middle Ages rather than in 2009, considering the way it continues to hit mosques with such precision. It's as if it is concentrating on a personal holy war against all the Muslim places of worship in Gaza.

Yet another downpour of bombs hit Jabalia, and then the tanks came in. They, which had tormented the borders by day with their creaking, are now entering north-west Gaza and razing the houses, metre by metre. They're burying the past and the future, whole families and an entire population, illegitimately dismissed from its own land, a people who haven't found any form of shelter except for huts in refugee camps.

We rushed out here to Jabalia after another terrible menace showered down from the sky last Friday evening. Hundreds of leaflets were thrown out of the planes ordering the general evacuation of the refugee camp. This threat has unfortunately materialized. The most fortunate have managed to escape instantly, taking a few possessions with them – a TV, a DVD player, and a few pieces of memorabilia from the life that once existed in Palestine, a land lost about 60 years ago. The vast majority haven't found anywhere to go. They will face those tanks hankering after their lives with the only weapon the Palestinians have left, the dignity of dying with their heads held up high.

My companions and I are aware of the enormous risk we're coming up against – tonight more than any other night. But we're more at ease in the midst of this Gazan hell than relaxing in a metropolitan heaven in Europe or America, where people celebrating the New Year and aren't really aware of just how complicit they are with the butchering of all these innocent civilians.

Stay human.

Subject: Doctors with Wings: Arafa Abed Al-Dayem R.I.P.

Date: 5th January 2009

From: Vittorio Arrigoni

'To the innocent people of Gaza, our war is not against you but against Hamas. If they don't stop shooting rockets against us, you'll be in danger.' It's the transcription of a recording you can hear when answering the phone in Gaza just now. The Israeli Army is under the illusion that the Palestinians have no eyes or ears. No eyes to see that the bombs are hitting civilian targets almost exclusively, such as mosques (15, the last being the Omar Bin Abd Al-Azeez Mosque in Beit Hanoun), schools, universities, markets and hospitals. No ears to hear the cries of pain and terror of the children, innocent victims and yet – at the same time – the predetermined targets of each one of these bombings. According to hospital records, as I'm writing, 120 minors were struck by the bombs, 548 being the total death toll so far, in addition to 2,700 wounded and many, many more missing.

Two days ago, night time never came to the Red Crescent Hospital in the Jabalia refugee camp. Apache helicopters hovering constantly overhead shower us with luminescent devices, to the point that we could no longer tell the difference between day and night. The repeated cannon

4th January 2009: Palestinian medical staff carry a child injured
by bomb shrapnel in Beit Lahiya in the northern Gaza Strip
(AP/Fadi Adwan)

fire from a tank positioned less than a kilometre from the
hospital seriously cracked open the building's walls, but
it managed to stand more or less intact until morning.
Around 10 white phosphorous bombs were dropped on
the neighbouring field, with machine gun fire exploding all
around. To the doctors of the Red Crescent Hospital, this
was clearly a message from the Israeli Army ordering an
immediate evacuation (or face destruction). We moved
the wounded into other hospitals, and the operative
ambulance base is now on Al-Nady Street. The medical staff
sits on the sidewalk waiting for the calls that follow one
after the other, frantically.

For the first time since the Israeli attack started, I've actually seen corpses of members of the Palestinian Resistance. A handful of individuals, next to the hundreds of civilian victims, the numbers of whom have risen exponentially since the land attacks started. Following the shooting at Jabalia Mosque, which left 11 dead and about 50 wounded and all of which took place while the tanks were coming in, for the whole of Saturday on board the ambulances we realized just how terrifyingly powerful the howitzers shot by the Israeli tanks were, as if destructive power had been lacking in the previous few days.

In Beit Hanoun, a family huddled in front of a wood stove in their house, was struck by one such killer cannon shot. We carried 15 wounded away, four of whom were in a hopeless condition. Later, towards 3.30am, we replied to an emergency call, but we ended up being too late. Standing by their front door, three women in tears handed us a four-year-old girl wrapped in a white sheet, her shroud – she was stone cold by then. Another family was hit in full, this time by the Air Force in Jabalia – with two adults injured by shrapnel. Their two children were only slightly hurt, but from their screaming it was obvious they were suffering from psychological trauma, something they would carry with them for the rest of their lives, an injury much deeper than a cut on the cheek. Even though no one ever remembers to mention them, there are thousands of children suffering from serious mental illnesses caused by the terror of constant bombing, or, worse, by the sight of their parents or siblings being torn apart by the explosions.

The crimes that Israel is staining its bloodied hands with in these hours go well beyond the boundaries of what can be imagined. The soldiers actually prevent us from running to the aid of the survivors in this immense unnatural catastrophe. When the wounded are close to the armoured vehicles they were just attacked by, we, in our Red Crescent ambulances, aren't allowed anywhere near, as the soldiers take potshots at us. Before we can hope to run in aid of any human lives, we need to be escorted by at least one Red Cross ambulance, thanks to an agreement of the latter with the Israeli Army's senior command. Just try and imagine how long such proceedings take – a death sentence for all those awaiting transfusions or urgent care. This is even truer considering the Red Cross has its own wounded to care for, leaving them without a chance of answering our every call. We must thus park in a 'protected' area, this term being a euphemism in Gaza, and wait for people to *bring us* their languishing relatives, often carrying them on foot.

That's what happened around 5.30 this morning. We stopped the ambulance with the engine on, in the middle of a crossing, communicating our whereabouts via phone to the relatives of some patients on their way. After 10 unnerving minutes, when we'd already decided to evacuate the area in response to another call, we noticed them as they turned the corner, advancing towards us slowly, a mule-drawn cart carrying some people. It turned out to be a couple and their two children. The best possible illustration of this non-war. This isn't really a war. There aren't two armies battling it out on one front, but a people enduring a siege by an Air Force, a Navy, and

5th January 2009: A man's rage as he carries a girl killed during an
Israeli attack on Al-Shifa Hospital in Gaza City (AP/Khalil Hamra)

what is now one of the world's most powerful infantries,
certainly the most technologically advanced when it
comes to military equipment. Here they are, attacking a
miserable strip of land, just 360 square kilometres, a place
where its inhabitants still use mules to move around, with
a hotchpotch resistance whose only real strength is their
readiness for martyrdom.

When that mule-drawn cart got close enough, we
approached them and beheld its macabre cargo with
horror. A child was lying with his skull cracked open, his
eyeballs literally hanging out of their sockets, swaying
onto his face like those at the end of a crab's stalks. When
we picked him up, he was still breathing. His little brother

had a disembowelled chest, and you could distinctly count his white ribs through the tatters of his torn flesh. Their mother pressed her hands on to that eviscerated chest, as if trying to fix what the fruit of her love had managed to create, and which the anonymous hatred of a soldier, obeying orders, had now forever destroyed. Yet another crime I want to report, and our umpteenth personal mourning.

The Israeli Army continues to target the ambulances. After the butchering of the doctor and nurse in Jabalia four days ago, today's new victim was a friend of ours: 35-year-old Arafa Abed Al-Dayem, a father of four. Around 8.30 yesterday morning, we received a call from Gaza City. Two civilians had been struck down by a tank's machine-gun fire. One of our Red Crescent ambulances rushed to their aid. Arafa and one of the nurses were loading the two wounded onto the ambulance and, while shutting the ambulance doors, they were hit by a howitzer from a tank.

The shot decapitated one of the wounded and also killed our friend. Nader, the nurse accompanying them, managed to survive although he is now a patient in the same hospital that he works in. Arafa, an elementary school teacher, was a voluntary paramedic in emergencies. We were being showered with bombs and, yet, hadn't had the heart to call Arafa in such a high-risk situation. He showed up of his own accord, working with a full awareness of the risks involved, convinced as he was that, aside from his family, there were other human beings in need of protection and aid. We miss his jokes, his irresistible and contagious sense of humour, and a balm for the soul in our bleakest moments.

Someone has to stop this massacre. In the last few days I've seen things, heard uproars and smelt pestilential miasmas that I'll never have the courage to talk about, if I should ever have children of my own. Is there anyone out there? The desolation of feeling isolated and abandoned is equivalent to a view of a Gaza neighbourhood after a heavy air raid campaign. Saturday evening, I was connected via phone to the protesting crowds in Milan, and I handed my cell phone over to the heroic doctors and nurses I'm working with at the moment. They looked reassured for a few moments. Demonstrations the world over are a sign that you can still believe in someone, but these demonstrations are still not large enough to exercise the necessary pressure on Western governments, which should be forcing Israel into a corner, making it take responsibility for its war crimes and crimes against humanity.

Many terrified pregnant women are prematurely giving birth right now. I was personally present with three of them as they were rushed to the delivery room. One of these, Samira, seven months pregnant, gave birth to a beautiful, tiny baby called Ahmed. Rushing to the Al-Auda Hospital on board the ambulance with her and leaving behind in our rear-view mirror the scenarios of death and destruction (the places where just a moment before we'd been picking up corpses), I thought for a moment that this new life, on the point of blossoming, could be a harbinger for future hope and peace. But the illusion melted away with the first rocket from the centre of Jabalia falling by the side of our ambulance. These brave mothers sadly give birth to creatures who take in nothing but the military green of tanks and jeeps or the blinking flashes that precede an explosion. What kind of adults will they grow up to be?

Stay human.

Subject: Al-Nakba

Date: 6th January 2009

From: Vittorio Arrigoni

They parade in fear, their eyes turned upwards, sur-
rendering to the sky which keeps raining terror and
death down upon them, and fearing the earth that keeps
shaking under them with every step they take, craters
opening up where there were once houses, schools,
universities, markets and hospitals. I've seen caravans
of desperate Palestinians evacuate Jabalia, Beit Hanoun
and all the refugee camps in Gaza, crowding the United
Nations' schools like earthquake survivors, like the victims
of a tsunami eating into the Gaza Strip and its civilian
population, without pity or compliance with human rights
and the Geneva Conventions. Most of all, without a single
Western government lifting a finger to stop this massacre,
or sending medical staff out here, or stopping the genocide
that Israel is smearing its hands with in these hours.

The indiscriminate attacks against the hospitals and their
medical staff continue. Yesterday, after having left the Al-
Auda Hospital in Jabalia, I received a call from Alberto, a
Spanish colleague with the ISM. A bomb had been dropped
there and Abu Mohammed, a nurse, had been seriously
injured to his head. Just moments before, in front of a
café, I'd been listening to the stories of the heroic deeds of

29

the communist Abu Mohammed's heroes, the leaders of the Popular Front: George Habbash, Abu Ali Mustafa and Ahmad Al-Sadat. His eyes lit up when I told him that the first understanding of Palestine and its immense tragedy had been passed onto me by my parents, both communists through and through. He asked me who'd been the truly revolutionary leaders of the Italian left, and I'd replied, 'Antonio Gramsci'. As for those of the present-day, I'd said I'd think it over and tell him the next day. But Abu Mohammed now lies in a coma, in the same hospital where he works. He spared himself my disappointing reply.

Towards midnight I received another call, from Eva this time – the building she was in was under attack. I know that building well: it's in downtown Gaza City. I'd once spent the night there along with some Palestinian photojournalists, whose job it is to try and capture through images and words something of the unnatural catastrophe we've been enduring these last 10 days. Reuters, Fox News, Russia Today and many, many other local or foreign agencies were under fire from seven rockets shot by an Israeli helicopter. They managed to evacuate everyone in time before anyone could be seriously injured – all those cameramen, photographers, reporters – all Palestinian, given that Israel won't allow any international journalists into Gaza. There are no 'strategic' targets around that building, nor a resistance fighting off the deadly armoured Israeli vehicles, currently located only a long way away towards the north.

Clearly, someone in Tel Aviv cannot bear the images of the massacres of civilians clashing with those briefings the Israeli officers provide, while offering mercenary journalists their aperitifs. These press conferences are persuading the world that the bombing targets are solely targeting Hamas terrorists, not one of those atrociously mutilated children we pull out of the rubble every day. In Zeitoun, about 10 kilometres from Jabalia, a bombed building crumbled over a family, leaving about 10 dead. The ambulances had to wait several hours before they could reach the spot, as the military persist in shooting at us. They shoot at ambulances and bomb hospitals. A few days ago, while I was being interviewed live on a well-known Milanese radio station, an Israeli 'pacifist' clearly spelt out to me that this was a war where both sides used all the weapons at their disposal. I then invited Israel to drop one of its many atomic bombs upon us, those they keep secretly stashed away, defying all treaties against nuclear proliferation. Why not just drop that decisive bomb of theirs and put an end to the inhuman agony of thousands of bodies, lying in tatters in the overcrowded hospital wards that I visit?

I took some black-and-white photos yesterday, the caravans of mule-drawn carts, overloaded beyond belief with children waving white drapes pointing skywards, their faces pale and terrified. Looking through those snaps of fleeing refugees today, shivers went down my spine. If they could only be superimposed with those portraying the Nakba of 1948, the Palestinian catastrophe, they would be the perfect mirror image of them. The cowardly passiveness of self-styled democratic states and governments are responsible for a new catastrophe in full swing, a new Nakba, a brand new ethnic cleansing befalling the Palestinian population right now.

Until a few moments ago we counted 650 dead, 153 murdered children, in addition to 3,000 injured, and innumerable missing. The number of civilian deaths in Israel has thankfully remained at four. But after this afternoon the death toll on the Palestinian side requires an urgent recount, ever since the Israeli Army has started attacking the United Nations schools, the very same that had been offering shelter to the thousands evacuated under threat of an imminent attack. They chased them out of the refugee camps, the villages, only to collect them all in one place, an easier target. Three schools were attacked today, the last being at Al-Fakhura, in Jabalia, which was hit smack bang in the middle. Over 80 dead: in a heartbeat, men, women, elderly people and children were wiped away, who believed themselves to be safe within those blue-tinted walls adorned by a United Nations logo.

The people sheltered within the other 20 UN schools are now shaking with fear. There's no way out anywhere in the Gaza Strip. This isn't Lebanon, where the civilians in the southern villages targeted by the Israeli bombs could flee to the north, or to Syria or Jordan. From being one enormous open-air prison, the Gaza Strip has become a deadly trap. We look at one another in bewilderment and ask ourselves whether the UN Security Council will finally and unanimously condemn these attacks after their own schools have been targeted. Someone out there has really decided to turn this place into a desert, and then call it peace.

A long night on the ambulances awaits us now, even though the arrival of dawn has become nothing but an illusion around here. Antenna towers all along the Strip have been destroyed and we've stopped relying on them for our mobile phones. I hope I may one day be able to see all the friends I can no longer contact, but I'm under no illusions. Bar none, everyone in Gaza is a walking target. The Italian Consulate has just contacted me, saying that tomorrow they'll evacuate a fellow Italian, an elderly nun who'd lived near the Catholic church in Gaza for the last 20 years, and who had by now been adopted by the Palestinians in the Strip. The consul gently urged me to seize this last opportunity and escape from this hell with the nun. I thanked him for the offer, and told him I'm not moving from here – I just can't. For the sake of the losses we endured, before being Italian, Spanish, British or Australian, right now we are all Palestinian. If only we could do that for just one minute a day, the way we were all Jewish during the Holocaust, I think we would have been spared this entire massacre.

Stay human.

27th December 2008: Gaza City. Some wounded locals wait
to be treated at Al-Shifa Hospital, the main hospital in the Gaza Strip
(Mohammed Al-Zaanoun and Majdi Fathi)

Subject: Slingshots vs. White Phosphorous Bombs

Date: 7th January 2009

From: Vittorio Arrigoni

'Take some kittens, some tender little moggies in a box', said Jamal, a surgeon at Al-Shifa, Gaza's main hospital, while a nurse actually placed a couple of bloodstained cardboard boxes in front of us. 'Seal it up, then jump on it with all your weight and might, until you feel their little bones crunching, and you hear the last muffled little mew.' I stared at the boxes in astonishment, and the doctor continued: 'Try to imagine what would happen after such images were circulated. The righteous outrage of public opinion, the complaints of the animal rights organizations....' The doctors went on in this vein, and I was unable to take my eyes off the boxes at our feet. 'Israel trapped hundreds of civilians inside a school as if in a box, including many children, and then crushed them with all the might of its bombs. What were the world's reactions? Almost nothing. We would have been better off as animals rather than Palestinians, we would have been better protected.'

At this point the doctor leans towards one of the boxes, and takes its lid off in front of me. Inside it are the amputated limbs, legs and arms, some from the knee down, others with the entire femur attached, from amputees injured at the Al-Fakhura United Nations school in Jabalia, which resulted in more than 50 casualties. Pretending to be taking an urgent call, I took my leave of Jamal, actually rushing to the bathroom to throw up. A little earlier I'd been involved in a conversation with Dr. Abdel, an ophthalmologist, regarding the rumours that the Israeli Army had been showering us with non-conventional weapons, forbidden by the Geneva Convention, such as cluster bombs and white phosphorous. The very same that the Israeli Army used during the last Lebanese war, as well as the US Air Force in Falluja, in violation of international norms.

In front of Al-Awda Hospital we witnessed and filmed white phosphorous bombs being used about 500 metres from where we stood, too far away to be absolutely certain there were any civilians underneath the Israeli Apaches, but so terribly close all the same. The Geneva Treaty of 1980 forbids white phosphorous being used directly as a war weapon in civilian areas, allowing it only as a smoke screen or for lighting. There's no doubt that using this weapon in Gaza, a strip of land concentrating the highest population rate in the world, is a crime all on its own.

Doctor Abdel told me that at Al-Shifa Hospital they don't have the medical and military competence to say for sure whether the wounds they examined on certain corpses were indeed caused by illegal weapons. But he gave his word that, in 20 years on the job, he had never seen casualties like these that were now being carried into the ward. He told me about the traumas to the skull, with the fractures to the vomer bone, the jaw, the cheekbones, the tear ducts, the nasal and palatine bones, all showing signs of the collision of an immense force against the victim's face. What he finds inexplicable is the total lack of eyeballs, which ought to leave a trace somewhere within the skull even with such a violent impact. Instead, we see Palestinian corpses coming into the hospitals without any eyes at all, as if someone had removed them surgically before handing them over to the coroner.

Israel has let us know that we've been generously granted a three-hour daily ceasefire, from 1.00 to 4.00pm. These statements from the Israeli military leadership are considered by the people of Gaza as having the same reliability as the Hamas leaders' declarations that they've just provoked a massacre of enemy soldiers. Just to be clear on this point, Tel Aviv's worst enemy is the very same that fights under the Star of David. Yesterday, a warship off the coast of Gaza's port picked out a large group of alleged guerrilla fighters from the Palestinian Resistance, moving as a united front around Jabalia. They shot their cannons at them. But as it turned out, they were their own fellow soldiers, with the shooting resulting in three being killed and about 20 injured.

No one here believes in the ceasefires that Israel calls, and as it happens, today at 2.00pm, Rafah was under attack by Israeli helicopters. There was also yet another massacre of children in Jabalia: three little sisters aged two, four and six from the Abed Rabbu family were slaughtered. Just half-an-hour earlier in Jabalia, once again the Red Crescent Hospital's ambulances were under attack. Eva and Alberto, my ISM companions were on board that ambulance and managed to film everything, passing those videos and photos on to all the major media.

Hassan was kneecapped, fresh from mourning the death of his friend Araf, a paramedic who was killed two days ago as he was going in aid of the injured in Gaza City. They had stopped to pick up the body of a man languishing in the middle of the road, when they were showered by about 10 shots from an Israeli sniper. One bullet hit Hassan in the knee and the ambulance was filled with holes. We're now at a death toll of 688, in addition to 3,070 injured, 158 dead children and countless missing. Only yesterday, we counted 83 dead, 80 of whom were civilians. Thankfully, the death toll on the Israeli side is still only at four.

Travelling towards Al-Quds Hospital, where I'll be working all night on the ambulances, I raced along on board one of the very few fearless taxi drivers left, zigzagging to avoid the bombs, and, on the corner of one street, I saw a group of dirty street urchins in tattered clothes, looking exactly like the 'sciuscià' kids of the Italian post-war period. They threw stones towards the sky with slingshots, at a remote and unreachable enemy toying with their lives. This is a crazy metaphor, which could serve as a snapshot of the absurdity of this place at the moment.

Stay human.

Subject: 'I won't leave my country!'

Date: 8th January 2009

From: Vittorio Arrigoni

My toothpaste, toothbrush, razors and shaving foam. The clothes I'm wearing, the cough medicine I'm using to get rid of a persistent cough, the cigarettes I bought for Ahmed, and some tobacco for my arghile. My cell phone, the laptop onto which I compulsively type eyewitness accounts from the hell surrounding me. All that's needed for a modest, yet dignified, existence in Gaza comes from Egypt, and arrives onto the shop shelves through the tunnels. These are the very same tunnels that the Israeli F16s haven't stopped bombing heavily in the last 12 hours, destroying thousands of Rafah houses near the border.

A few months ago I had three dodgy teeth fixed, and at the end of the operation I asked my Palestinian dentist where he'd gotten all of his dental equipment from – the anaesthetic, the syringes, the ceramic inlays and all the other tools. With a sly look on his face, he'd made a certain gesture with his hands: from underground. There's no doubt that explosives and weapons were also smuggled through the tunnels underneath Rafah, the very same that the resistance is using today to try and contain the terrifying advance of the Israeli tanks. But it's next to nothing compared with the tonnes of consumer goods flowing into famished Gaza under this criminal siege. It's easy enough to find photos on the web showing how even livestock comes in from Egypt through the tunnels. Sedated, strapped-up goats and cows are lowered into an Egyptian well, re-emerging on this side to provide milk, cheese and meat. Even the main hospitals in the Strip stock up surreptitiously at the border. The tunnels were the only means by which the Palestinians could survive the siege. Long before the current bombing, this siege became the cause of a 60% unemployment rate, forcing 80% of families to live off humanitarian handouts.

Our ISM colleagues in Rafah describe the umpteenth mass exodus they've witnessed: caravans of desperate refugees leaving their homes for Egypt, on mule-drawn carts or hodgepodge vehicles. A déjà-vu scenario. In recent days, leaflets were raining down from the planes, intimidating the Palestinians into evacuating. Since Israel always keeps her threatening promises, bombs are now pouring down from her planes.

Today's new homeless will spend the night with their relatives, friends or acquaintances in Gaza. After yesterday's massacre in Jabalia, no one dares take shelter in the United Nations schools anymore. But a considerable number haven't gone anywhere, as they have nowhere safe to go. They shall be spending the night praying to God that they'll be spared, since no one on earth seems to take any interest whatsoever in their existence. The death toll at present is of 768 Palestinians, with 3,129 wounded, and 219 children dead. The count of civilian victims on the Israeli side is thankfully still only four.

27th December 2008: Gaza City. A child waits in front of one of the few bakeries still open, but the flour is running out and the people of Gaza are forced to do without bread for many days (Mohammed Al-Zaanoun and Majdi Fathi)

In Zeitoun, a neighbourhood East of Gaza City, the Red Cross ambulances could only rush to the scene of a massacre after several hours, with permission from the Israeli military leadership. When they finally got there, they picked up 17 corpses and 10 injured, all belonging to the Al-Samouni family. It was a perfect execution: in the tiny bodies of the children it was possible to notice bullet holes rather than wounds caused by shrapnel.

The last two nights in the Gaza City hospitals were quieter than usual, as we assisted a number of injured in the dozens rather than in the hundreds. Obviously after the massacre at the Al-Fakhura school, the Israeli Army surpassed the daily total of civilian casualties as an offering to its bloodthirsty government in view of the imminent elections. We have a feeling though that the morgues will be filled to bursting point again tonight.

With our sirens screaming, we continue to rush pregnant women into hospital as they give birth prematurely. It's as if nature and the conservation instinct were inducing these brave mothers to pre-empt the due-date of these newly-born, making up for the growing number of the dead. The first cries of the newborn, when they survive, can, only for a moment, rise over the rumbling of the bombs.

Leila, a colleague at the ISM, asked our neighbours' children to write some of their impressions of the atrocious tragedy we're enduring. Here are some extracts of their words, the horrors of war seen through the pure and innocent gaze of Gaza's children:

Suzanne, aged 15: 'Life in Gaza is very difficult. Actually we can't describe everything. We can't sleep, we can't go to school and study. We feel a lot of feelings, sometimes we feel afraid and worry because the planes and the ships, they hit [us] twenty-four hours [a day]. Sometimes we feel bored because there is no electricity during the day, and in the night, it comes for just four hours and when it comes we are watching the news on TV. And we see kids and women who are injured and dead. So we live under siege and war.'

Fatma, aged 13: 'It was the hardest week in our lives. The first day we were to school, having the final exam of the first term, then the explosions started, and many students were killed and injured, and the others surely lost a relative or a neighbour. There's no electricity, no food, no bread. What can we do? It's the Israelis! All the people in the world celebrated the New Year; we also celebrate but in a different way.'

Sara, aged 11: 'Gaza is living under a siege, like a big jail: no water, no electricity. People feel afraid, [they] don't sleep at night, and every day more people are killed. Until now, more than 400 are killed and more than 2,000 injured. And students had their final first-term exams, so Israel hit the Ministry of Education, and a lot of ministries. Every day people are asking, "When will it end?", and they are waiting for more ships with activists like Vittorio and Leila.'

Darween, aged 8: 'I am a Palestinian kid: I won't leave my country, so I will have lots of advantages, because I won't leave my country, and I hear a sound of rockets, so I won't leave my country.'

Meriam is four. Her siblings asked her, 'What do you feel when you hear the rockets?' And she said, 'I'm scared!', before running to take cover behind her father's legs.

Sadly, Gaza has been shrouded in obscurity these last 10 days. I can recharge my computer and phone only in the hospitals. We watch TV with the doctors and paramedics while waiting for an urgent call. We listen to the rumblings in the distance, and after a few minutes the Arab satellite networks report exactly where the explosions took place. We often watch ourselves pull bodies out of the rubble, as if having seen it all in the flesh weren't enough already. Last night I switched over to an Israeli channel with the remote. They were showing a traditional music festival, complete

43

with scantily-clad showgirls and firework displays at the end. We went back to our horror, not on screen, but in the ambulances. Israel has every right to laugh and sing even while they're massacring their neighbours. Palestinians only ask to die a different kind of death, say, of old age.

Stay human.

Subject: Killing Hippocrates

Date: 9th January 2009

From: Vittorio Arrigoni

In Gaza, a firing squad put Hippocrates up against a wall, aimed and fired. The absurd declarations of an Israeli secret services' spokesman, according to which the army was given the green light to fire at ambulances because they allegedly carried terrorists, is an illustration of the value that Israel assigns to human life these days – the lives of their enemies, that is. It's worth revisiting what's stated in the Hippocratic Oath, which every doctor swears before practising their profession. The following passages are especially worthy of note: 'I solemnly pledge myself to consecrate my life to the service of humanity. I will practise my profession with conscience and dignity. The health and life of my patient will be my first consideration. I will cure all patients with the same diligence and commitment. I will not permit considerations of religion, nationality, race, party politics, or social standing to intervene between my duty and my patient.'

Nine doctors and voluntary nurses have been killed since the start of the bombing campaign, and about 10 ambulances were shot at by the Israeli artillery. The survivors are quaking with fear, but refuse to take a step back. The crimson flashes of the ambulances are the only

27th December 2008: Gaza City. Bombing in the northern part of the city (Mohammed Al-Zaanoun and Majdi Fathi)

bursts of light in the dark streets of Gaza, bar the flashes that precede an explosion. Regarding these crimes, the last report comes from Pierre Wettach, Head of the Red Cross in Gaza. His ambulances had access to the site of a massacre, in Zeitoun (east of Gaza City) only 24 hours after an Israeli attack. The rescue workers state that they found themselves facing a blood-curdling scenario. 'In one of the houses four small children were found near the body of their dead mother. They were too weak to stand on their feet. We also found a grown man, also too weak to stand upright. About 20 corpses were found lying on mattresses.' The witnesses to this umpteenth massacre describe how the Israeli soldiers, after arriving in the neighbourhood, gathered the numerous members of the Al-Samouni family into one building and then proceeded to bomb it repeatedly.

My ISM companions and I have been driving around in the Red Crescent ambulances for days, suffering many attacks and losing a dear friend, Arafa, who was struck by a howitzer shot from a cannon. A further three paramedics, all friends, are presently inpatients at the very same hospitals they worked in just a few days ago. Our duty on the ambulances is to rescue the injured, not to carry guerrilla fighters. When we find someone lying in the street in a pool of their own blood, we don't have the time to check their papers or ask them whether they support Hamas or Fatah. Most of the seriously injured can't talk, much like the dead.

A few days ago, while picking up a badly-wounded patient, another man with light injuries tried to hop onto the ambulance. We pushed him out, just to make it clear to whoever's watching from up above that we don't serve as a taxi to carry members of the resistance around. Last night at Al-Quds Hospital in Gaza City, seventeen-year-old Miriam was carried in, in full-blown labour. Her father and sister-in-law, both dead, had passed through the hospital in the morning, both victims of the indiscriminate bombing. Miriam gave birth to a gorgeous baby during the night, not aware of the fact that while she lay in the delivery room, her young husband had arrived in the morgue one floor below her.

In the end, even the United Nations has started to see that we're all in the same boat here in Gaza. We're all

47

walking targets for the snipers. The death toll is now at 789 dead, 3,300 wounded (with 410 in critical condition), 230 children killed and countless missing. The death toll on the Israeli side has thankfully remained at four. John Ging, Director of UNRWA's (United Nations Relief and Works Agency for Palestine Refugees) Field Operations in Gaza, has related the UN announcement that they'll suspend their humanitarian activities in the Gaza Strip. I bumped into Ging at the Ramattan press office and saw him wagging his finger with disdain at Israel before the cameras. The UN stopped its work in Gaza after two of its operators were killed yesterday, ironically during the three-hour ceasefire that Israel had announced and, as usual, had failed to stick to. 'The civilians in Gaza have three hours a day at their disposal in which to survive, the Israeli soldiers have the remaining 21 in which to try and exterminate them', I heard Ging state, two steps away from me.

Yasmine, the wife of one of the many journalists waiting in line at the Erez Pass, wrote to me from Jerusalem. Israel won't grant these journalists a pass to let them in and film or describe the immense unnatural catastrophe that has befallen us in the last 13 days. She said: 'The day before yesterday I went to have a look at Gaza from the outside. The world's journalists are all huddled on a small sandy hill a few kilometres from the border. Innumerable cameras are pointed towards us. Planes circle overhead – you can hear them but you can't see them. They're like hallucinations, like something in your head until you see the black smoke rising from the horizon, in Gaza. The hill has also become a tourist site for Israelis in the area. With their large binoculars and cameras, they come and watch the bombings live.'

While I write this piece of correspondence in a mad rush, a bomb has been dropped on to the building next to the one I'm in right now. The windowpanes shake, my ears ache, I look out the window and see that the building holding the major Arabic media agencies has been struck. It's one of Gaza City's tallest buildings, the Al-Jawhara building. A camera crew is permanently stationed on the roof, and I can now see them all waving their arms and asking for help as they're covered by a black cloud of smoke.

Paramedics and journalists, the most heroic occupations in this corner of the world. Yesterday I paid Tamim a visit at the Al-Shifa Hospital – he's a journalist who's survived an air raid. He explained how he thinks that Israel is adopting the same, identical terrorist techniques as Al-Qaeda: bombing a building, waiting for the journalists and ambulances to rush in, then dropping another bomb to finish the latter off as well. In his view that's why there've been so many casualties among the journalists and paramedics. As he said this, the nurses around his bed all nodded in agreement. Smilingly, Tamim showed me his two stubs for legs. He was happy he was still around to tell the story, while his colleague, Mohammed, had died with a camera in his hand when the second explosion had proved fatal. In the meantime I asked about the bomb that had just been dropped on the building next door, where two journalists, both Palestinian, one from Libyan TV and the other from Dubai Television, have been injured. This is a harsh new reminder that this massacre must in no way be described or recorded. All that's left for me to hope is that among the Israel's military leaders no one reads *Il Manifesto*, or habitually visits my blog.

Stay human.

Subject: Total Destruction: Work in Progress

Date: 10th January 2009

From: Vittorio Arrigoni

Some Palestinian families have handed us some leaflets that had fallen from the sky in the last few days, courtesy of the Israeli Air Force, in lieu of the customary bombs. The first leaflet, translated from the Arabic, reads:

> To all the people living in this area. Due to the terror-
> ist acts with which the terrorists from your area are
> attacking Israel, the Israeli Army Forces were forced
> to take immediate action in your area. We thus urge
> you, for your own safety, to immediately evacuate the
> area. The Israeli Army.

In short, the Israelis are sticking a 'work in progress' note on every door, before razing whole neighbourhoods to their foundations, and forever dashing hopes of a life in the present or in the future. Apparently, those who haven't got anywhere to flee to are consigned to be buried under tonnes of rubble. A little while ago they had warned us they intended to throw more leaflets, threatening us with a 'third phase of war of terror [that] is about to start'. Israeli military commanders are indeed polite – they ask the population of Gaza to cooperate before crushing them like insects.

If the leaflets aren't persuasive enough, it's up to the Air Force to knock gently on the roofs of Gaza's houses. It's a brand new tactic – slightly less powerful bombs are dropped, though powerful enough to tear the roofs clear off the houses, 'gently' persuading their occupiers to evacuate them. After two or three minutes the planes drift past again, and nothing remains of the buildings. Where should the evacuees go? There are no safe shelters in the whole of the Strip, and personally I fear for my own life more when walking past a mosque or a school, than when standing in front of any of the government buildings, which are still standing intact. Last night, 20 metres from my home, Israeli jet fighters tore down the fire station. This morning, on the street running parallel to the port, I discovered some craters several metres deep, as if meteors had rained down from the sky, as are often featured in sci-fi movies. The difference here is that the special effects are pretty damn painful.

Visiting the wards of Al-Shifa Hospital, crowded with injured patients awaiting treatment, you can bump into a doctor who doesn't look very Arab. Mads Gilbert is a Norwegian doctor from the NGO Norwac. Gilbert, an anaesthetist, confirms our suspicion regarding the use of forbidden weapons by Israel on Gaza's civilians: 'Many injured arrive with extreme amputations, with both their legs reduced to a pulp, which I suspect is an effect of Dime weapons.'[1] This is happening while Navi Pillay, UN High Commissioner for

---

1. The Dime (Dense Inert Metal Explosive) Bomb is an innovative explosive made with a warhead of carbon and epoxy resin integrated with steel and tungsten. This explosive was designed for urban guerrilla warfare, and was made to strike specific targets and cause as much damage as possible.

10th January 2009: A woman carrying her possessions amidst the rubble of a refugee camp in the southern Gaza Strip, destroyed by an Israeli air raid (AP/Khalid Omar)

Human Rights, reports that 'extremely serious violations possibly constituting war crimes' are taking place.

The last instance of one such crime happened a few hours ago, east of Jabalia, where a family, at the point of evacuating their house, was stocking up on some food supplies at a small shop. When it was promptly bombed, eight were killed, and all members of the Abed Rabbu family, in addition to two others, were left severely injured. People I speak to in the street are under the impression that Israel is biding its time, even while the bombs are being dropped non-stop and the land artillery is slowly advancing. The soldiers have no problems in stocking up with 'K-rations', the individual military food rations, unlike many people in Gaza who can no longer get any bread. The bakers, having run out of flour, have resorted to mixing it with animal flour with which to make buns. It's week-old bread, green with mould. You cook it over a small fire lit with a couple of pieces of wood and I can assure you that, even then, it's not exactly a delicacy.

All over the net, Israel is uploading dozens of films featuring bird's eye-view images, allegedly showing how precise its bombings against the 'terrorists' are, or against hypothetical enemy warehouses stocking weapons and explosives. The dizzying count of civilian casualties is enough to discredit these videos. I wonder how Israel can call itself civilized and democratic, when its army, in trying to drive out and kill an enemy, won't hesitate to knock down an entire, crowded building, burying dozens of innocent victims alive in the process. It's as if the Italian army hunting down a dangerous mafia criminal started heavily bombing the centre of Palermo.

As sit here I writing this, there are 821 Palestinians dead, 93 being women, and 235 children. Twelve paramedics were killed while fulfilling their duty and three journalists died with cameras hanging round their necks. A good 3,350 are among the injured, with more than half being under 18 years of age. According to the Al-Mezan Center for Human Rights based in Jabalia, renowned for its reliability, they make up 85% of the Palestinian civilian casualties massacred in the last two weeks. The death toll on the Israeli side has thankfully remained at four.

If the United Nations cannot protect the Palestinian civilian population from the massive Israeli violations of their own international humanitarian obligations, my friends from the Free Gaza Movement will give it a shot, ready as they are to sail to Gaza in a few days. Among them are doctors, nurses and human rights activists, who consider it their personal moral duty to do whatever is humanly possible to provide some measure of protection. They had already tried to get here on the 31st December, on board the *Dignity*. But the Israeli Navy had rammed our boat in international waters, trying to sink it, and had subsequently spoken of 'an accident'. I will wait for my friends with their load of humanitarian aid among the ruins of what's left of the port. Here's to hoping that no more 'accidents' will occur off the coast this time.

The second leaflet dropped from planes that we've translated is a scream:

> Citizens of Gaza, take responsibility for your destiny! In Gaza the terrorists and those who launch rockets against Israel represent a threat to your lives and to those of your families. If you wish to help your families and brothers in Gaza, all you'll have to do is call the number below and give us information on the whereabouts of those responsible for launching rockets. The terrorist militia has turned you into the first victims of their actions. Avoiding more atrocities being committed is now your responsibility! Don't hesitate! Complete discretion is guaranteed. You can contact us at the following number: 02-5839749. Otherwise write to us at the following email, giving us any information you may have on terrorist activities: *helpgaza2008@gmail.com*.

Many write to me from Italy, filled with frustration at not being able to do anything about the genocide currently taking place. I would urge you to continue showing your indignation and supporting human rights. If you then have five minutes to spare and a phone card, the details contained in the last leaflet could come in useful in communicating your disdain to those who cynically gamble with the lives of a million-and-a-half people via air, sea and land. Never would a phone card have been better spent. Those 235 massacred children are asking for it.

Stay human.

Subject: Vultures and Bounty Hunters

Date: 12th January 2009

From: Vittorio Arrigoni

We still try to create routes of salvation via the sea, to make a breakthrough into this tormented land, now confiscated and imprisoned, every inch of it raped and reduced to a cemetery for corpses that are being denied a peaceful repose. For a few days now, even funerals have become the targets of the Israeli Air Force, as if murdered Palestinians deserve additional punishment in death as well.

If a humanitarian passage is struggling to make its way and come in aid of a people at the end of their tether, the *Spirit of Humanity*, one of our Free Gaza Movement boats, will try to be there for them. It sailed from Larnaca, Cyprus, today and will bring tonnes of medicine to Gaza's port, in addition to about 40 doctors, nurses, journalists, European parliamentarians, and human rights activists representing 17 different nations in all. Human beings, like myself, like many who vent their indignation, are ready to risk their lives rather than lounge passively in their living rooms watching news bulletins that reveal only a tiny fraction of what the massacre being inflicted upon us is doing here.

On the 29th December, my friends gave it a shot with *Dignity*, but they were attacked by the Israeli Navy. It tried to sink them. They had to send out an SOS and fled to Lebanon with engine failure and a leak in their hull. On that occasion it was only by pure chance that no one was badly hurt, so we hope human rights as well as the lives of the activists will be spared tomorrow. There are terrifying catastrophes in this world, such as earthquakes and hurricanes, inevitable natural phenomena. But Gaza endures an unnatural humanitarian catastrophe being perpetuated by Israel, damaging a people long reduced to abject poverty and submission. Gazans are a desperate people without bread or milk to feed their children. They no longer shed any tears when mourning, as their eyes are also on a strictly imposed diet. The entire world cannot ignore this tragedy and, if they continue to do so, we don't want any part of it. Every day we invoke someone above us to stop the genocide, but for tomorrow all we ask is for our small boat to land in Gaza with its cargo of compassion and empathy. May the Palestinians also receive the same rights that Israelis, or any other people on earth enjoy.

The sea can be an anchor of hope, or a scenario of destruction. According to the Ma'an Press Agency, with Reuters echoing their statement, the United States are about to ship 300 tonnes of weapons to Israel via cargo ships sailing from Greece. Weapons and enormous amounts of explosives and fuses, and all that's needed to raze thousands of houses to their foundations. There are 120,000 homeless displaced from Gaza to Jabalia already. But most, including many of my friends, haven't budged and have nowhere to flee. Journalists, doctors and gravediggers: for 16 days non-stop now these have been the busiest professionals in Gaza. The circling vultures that follow in the wake of the bomber planes stir up more hatred among the Palestinians, especially towards those seated where the late lamented Yasser Arafat (1929-2004), the former Chairman of the Palestianian Liberation Organisation, used to sit. They now itch to come and take over the throne towering over Gaza's ashes.

The death toll is now at 923, with 4,150 wounded, including 255 horrendously butchered Palestinian children. The number of dead on the Israeli side has thankfully stayed at four. Rumour has it that Ehud Olmert, the Israeli Prime Minister,[2] had told his side that hitting a death toll of 1,000 civilians marked the limit after which this brutal attack and infanticide would be halted. It's a bit like what happens at the Vucciria markets in Palermo, where quarters of beef are hung up to drip blood out in the open, and you haggle for the meat – so much per kilo.

Few Palestinians now miss tuning in for Ismail Haniyeh's[3] appearances on the small screen here in the Gaza Strip. You can't speak of a ceasefire without simultaneously establishing an end to the siege. Continuing to keep Gaza under siege now that it's been reduced to a heap of rubble, not allowing provisions and medicine to come through, preventing the sick and injured from getting out, is equivalent to condemning them to more prolonged agony. These in brief were the words spoken by Hamas's leader,

2. The successor to Olmert as Prime Minister was Benjamin Netanyahu, who took office on 31st March 2009.

3. Ismail Haniyeh (b. 1963) is a senior political leader of Hamas and became one of two Prime Ministers of the Palestinian National Authority in 2006. His dismissal as Prime Minister by President Mahmoud Abbas in 2007 has been the subject of political and legal dispute, although he has continued to act in an ex-officio capacity in Gaza.

27th December 2008: Al-Saraya, Gaza City. The ruins of main police station in Al-Suraya that had been bombed (Mohammed Al-Zaanoun and Majdi Fathi)

spoken from an underground bunker from God knows where. These words find an echo in Gazan public opinion. This was the speech of a leader who could have fled and taken refuge elsewhere. To the contrary, he decided to risk a bomb being dropped on his head like everyone else.

I was just interrupted, while typing this piece, by the usual intimidating phone call ordering us to evacuate the building before a bombing. I'm currently in the building where the main international media agencies operate, these being, among others, Al-Jazeera, Ramattan and Reuters. We were forced to unplug our PCs, rush downstairs and crowd the street, where we kept our eyes glued to the sky, trying to pick out where the destructive thunder would strike from this time. There won't be any cameras or reporters around to document the civilian massacre tonight, as we suspect that Gaza's innocent casualties will be more numerous than usual. Still standing in the street, I stared at Alberto, winking at him. He came up closer and, whispering, I asked him whether he thought it plausible that the threatening phone call had been made especially for the two of us, after the discovery of the American website singling us out as targets:

ALERT THE IDF MILITARY TO TARGET ISM

Number to call if you can pinpoint the locations of Hamas with their ISM members. From the US call, 011-972-2-5839749. From other countries drop the 011. Help us neutralize the ISM, now definitely a part of Hamas since the war has begun.

#1 ISM TARGET FOR THE ISRAELI AIR FORCE AND IDF GROUND TROOPS:

VITTORIO ARRIGONI (PICTURED BELOW) IS CURRENTLY IN GAZA ASSISTING HAMAS

This is copied from 'stoptheism.com'. Don't bother to visit this website or provide a link to it from your own websites. It's a sociological case to be passed on to future generations for study. On closer analysis of the present, the future will pronounce its sentence without appeal: of how hatred was the purest of all feelings. Spite against anything that's different could fuel whole armies, becoming the feeling that brings masses of people together. There's no need for my enemies and those who wish for my martyrdom to dial that number. The Israeli Army knows exactly where to find me tonight – on the Al-Quds Hospital ambulances in Gaza City.

Stay human.

Subject: Children of a Lesser God

Date: 14th January 2009

From: Vittorio Arrigoni

The children of a lesser God. I'm referring to the ones for whom the shelter of their mother or father's embrace has been permanently shattered by a thunderbolt from the sky. They continue to atone for the spite passed on from one generation to the next, through no fault of their own. The soldiers bearing the Star of David are perfectly at ease in their roles as so many contemporary Herods, with 253 massacred Palestinian children so far. An endless horror, for which no soldier, no Israeli army officer, nor the Israeli government have ever been forced to own up to. If these innocent victims are spared for a few hours, it might not necessarily be so for the buildings and courtyards providing a backdrop for their games, dreams and ambitions, their fantasies of growing up. The places filling the void left by their deceased fathers and mothers, that is, orphanages, have become a favourite nesting place for a species of Israeli mechanical bird. It's there that the fighter planes go and lay their bombs. My fellow ISM volunteers in Rafah have written to me, saying:

> On Sunday, 11th January, at about 3.00am, the F16s bombed the orphanage of the Dar al-Fadila Association, which included a school, a college, a computer centre and a mosque in Taha Hussein Street, in the Kherbat al-Adas neighbourhood, north-east of Rafah. Parts of the buildings were severely damaged. The school assisted 500 orphaned children.

This very personal Israeli jihad against Islam's sacred places along the Strip is still under way as well, with blessings from the international community's lack of anything resembling a protest. Including the Kherbat al-Adas Mosque, 20 Muslim places of worship have been razed to the ground up till now. Thankfully, no Qassam 'rocket' has as yet even brushed the walls of a synagogue. Otherwise, we're certain that we'd have heard rightful cries of disdain from every corner of the world. But it comes as no surprise to us that no one complains about this massive anti-Islamic campaign. God must be paying a tax for receiving prayers from the Palestinians.

Out of almost 950 victims, 85% are civilians. The infernal Israeli death machine is slowly advancing, taking over the whole of Gaza, knocking down houses, schools, universities, hospitals, without any tangible sign from the international community of a will to boycott these actions. It's now our turn, as ordinary citizens without citizenship (if not without the feeling of belonging to a human family), to try and get in the way of this hellish contraption.

I recently met Doctor Haidar Eid, a Professor at Al-Quds University in Gaza City. A leftist intellectual type, tough as nails and simultaneously good-humoured, passionate

11th January 2009: A boy stands amidst the rubble of a mosque and Islamic school destroyed by an Israeli missile in Rafah (AP/Eyad Baba)

and generous, the likes of which is completely extinct in Italy today. And if they're still to be found, their type is likely to be imprisoned in some basement, removed from the collective memory. It's impossible to adapt their type to the bipartisan trend whereby post-fascists and post-socialists walk arm in arm, reciting in unison their refrain to defend every single massacre Israel carries out. Haidar also happens to be a spokesman for PACBI (The Palestinian Campaign for the Academic and Cultural Boycott of Israel, website: *http://www.pacbi.org/*), and BNC (The Boycott, Divestment & Sanctions Campaign National Committee, website: *http://bdsmovement.net/*).

History is a teacher, but it has no students. Nelson Mandela or Mahatma Gandhi are at the moment unable to hold remedial lessons. Thankfully, the history lesson offered by South Africa's example can show us the way towards forcing a racist and colonialist Israel towards compromise. Refraining from boycotting the regime of apartheid back then was a little like being an accomplice to it. What has possibly changed today? Like myself, the vast majority of Palestinians don't think the answer to the Israeli occupation and the ongoing massacre is suicide bombings, 'kamikazes' and 'rockets' against Sderot. Boycotting is peaceful and non-violent, the most humanly acceptable answer to a conflict so depraved it has turned every gesture into something inhuman. It's the best weapon in our arsenal of non-violence, as Naomi Klein reminds us in the London *Guardian*.[4] Haidar even manages to look on the bright side despite the bloody pit we're sinking into. Just as the world felt the time had come to say 'Enough!' after the Sharpeville massacre of 21st March 1960 when three black citizens were torn to pieces by the will of a barbaric regime in South Africa, the incomparable massacre of 1,000 Palestinian civilians could breathe life into an equally strong activist campaign to punish Israeli crimes.

Haidar also supports the idea of Israel and Palestine as a sole, secular, democratic, and inter-religious state: he sees no other pragmatic way out of the conflict. More intimately, he speaks to me of Al-Nakba, which he was spared from by a few years, as if it had been very much brought to life by the stories he had inherited from his family. As the

---

4. 'Enough. It's time for a boycott', *Guardian*, 10th January 2009.

child of a post-catastrophe, he speaks without mincing his words. The Nakba has been passed down to him as a nightmare that has fed into the collective unconscious of thousands of Palestinians. The nightmare has come to life again, knocking on the rooftops on the 27th December. It still hasn't finished inflicting sleepless nights ever since. Haidar encourages me to divulge all this, so I jot down his appeal in my tattered notebook to no longer buy anything 'made in Israel'. You can pick out Israeli products on the shelves from their barcodes, with 729 being the first three numbers.

Get hold of a list and stick it on your fridge door for safe keeping until your next shopping trip. 'If you buy just one glass of water that was imported from Israel, you might be funding one of the bullets that might lodge itself into one of our children's bodies,' said Haidar.

The boycotting impetus that saw the light in Palestine in 2005 is now taking gigantic steps forward and is spreading among millions of consumers around the world. Venezuelan President Hugo Chavez, who expelled the Israeli Ambassador and stopped all relations with the state that's currently strangling us, is an example for all of our politicians to emulate.

The South African leaders of the struggle against apartheid, Nelson Mandela, Ronnie Kasrils and Desmond Tutu, have stated that Israel's oppression of Palestine is far worse than South Africa's of the blacks ever was. Some Israeli Jews have joined the boycotting campaign, about 500 so far, among them Ilan Pappé and Neta Golan, the descendent of Holocaust survivors, who protests, 'Never again!' The Israeli poet Aharon Shabtai also urges us to act:

My hopes rest on Europe's support, hoping that the descendents of Voltaire and Rousseau might help Israel, because Israel won't end its occupation until Europe says 'Enough!' Only pressure from civilized and democratic nations can change the situation and bring us peace. The current situation, with the army in charge, cannot be changed from the inside. For the values that it represents, Europe must refuse to continue cooperating with Israel. 729 must therefore become our Shoah: never again!

Stay human.

Subject: Jabalia's Circles of the Inferno

Date: 15th January 2009

From: Vittorio Arrigoni

Dante Alighieri could never have imagined circles as hellish as the wards of the damned in Jabalia's hospitals. The laws of divine justice are turned on their head around here: the more innocent the victim, the less likely that they'll be spared martyrdom through shelling. At Kamal Odwan and Al-Auda Hospitals, the ceramic tiles in the first aid units are always pristine. The cleaners are kept permanently busy wiping away the blood dripping copiously from the stretchers constantly being brought in carrying massacred bodies. Iyad Mutawwaq was walking in the street when a bomb tore open a building not far from him. He and other passers-by rushed over to try and help when a second bomb was dropped on the same building. It killed a father of nine, two brothers and another passer-by who had rushed over to help. The same story could be told over ten or a hundred times. The perfect terrorist technique is being carried out immaculately by the Israeli Army. You drop a bomb, wait for the first-aiders, then drop another bomb on the wounded and the people rushing in to help.

In Iyad's eyes, these were American bombs, but they also carry the stamp of Hosni Mubarak, the Egyptian dictator, who rivals Ehud Olmert here in Gaza when it comes to stirring up resentment. Behind Iyad's bed, an elderly man with both his arms in plasters is lying staring at the ceiling. I'm told he's lost everything, his family and his home. He stares at the cracks in the falling plaster, as if seeking an answer for the sheer destruction of his existence. Khaled worked in Israel for 25 years, prior to the first Intifada. In recognition, Tel Aviv hasn't even granted him a pension, only a series of missiles from land and air onto his house. He suffers from shrapnel wounds all over his body. I ask him where he plans to go after he's been discharged from hospital. He says he'll join his family, out on the streets.

Not unlike Khaled's family, many others don't know where to find shelter. The most fortunate were offered hospitality by relatives and acquaintances, but can you really say that 100 people crammed into two apartments having three rooms each is really a life? Two bombs were dropped onto Ahmed Jaber's home and though his family initially fled, it wasn't third time lucky for some of them. The third explosion buried seven of his relatives under the rubble, including two children aged eight and nine – plus his neighbour's children. He says:

> They made us leap back in time, back to 1948. This is their punishment for our attachment to our country. They can tear my arms and legs off from my body, but they won't make me leave my land.

A doctor takes me aside and tells me that Ahmed's seven-year-old daughter was just brought in, or what was left of her, inside a tiny cardboard box. They don't have the heart to tell him and make his already precarious health condition any worse. In the evening they took the phone away from Iyad as well, to prevent him from receiving any more bad news. A tank shell had hit his sister's house, beheading her in the process.

In the end, our Free Gaza Movement boat never got to the port in Gaza. About 100 miles from their designated destination, they were intercepted in international waters by four Israeli war ships, poised to open fire and kill its cargo of doctors, nurses and human rights activists. No one must dare to obstruct the massacre of civilians, now in full swing for the last three weeks. East of Jabalia, in front of the border, eyewitnesses speak of numerous decaying bodies in the streets. Their rotting flesh is being devoured by dogs. There are also hundreds of people unable to get anywhere, many of whom are injured. The ambulances simply cannot get anywhere near, with trigger-happy snipers all over the place. Palestinians are sick of languishing in the midst of this general indifference, and many even accuse the International Red Cross and the UN of not doing enough, including not fulfilling their duties, nor risking their lives to save hundreds. We of the ISM will thus equip ourselves with some stretchers and proceed on foot to the areas where humanity has surpassed all boundaries, eclipsing itself in the process.

The heavy-bottomed settlers sitting in the pristine lounges of armchair politics harp on about military strategies against Hamas. Meanwhile, we're being literally massacred out here. They bomb hospitals, and yet there are some who still champion Israel's right to self-defence. In any self-styled civilized country, self-defence is proportionate to the attack. In these 20 days we've counted 1,075 dead Palestinians, 85% of whom were civilians, and over 5,000 injured, of whom half were under 18 years of age. 303 children have been atrociously massacred. Thankfully, there were still only four victims on the Israeli side. It's equivalent to saying that for Israel, butchering at least 250 Palestinians is a justified bloodbath in avenging each civilian victim on its own side. How can this lop-sided reaction not take one back to some of modern European history's bleakest periods?

Let's get straight to the point: are we seriously talking about self-defence? For journalists who support the refrain that Hamas bears full responsibility for this genocide, as well as for breaking the truce between Israel and Palestine, I would like to remind them of the UN's position on the matter. Professor Richard Falk, a special rapporteur for human rights at the UN, has clearly expressed his views: it was in fact Israel that broke the ceasefire in November, by literally exterminating 17 Palestinians. In the same month, no Israeli victims had been recorded, none in October and none in the previous two months. We were also recently reminded of this by Nobel Peace Prize winner and ex-US President Jimmy Carter. It really is a crying shame that a journalist like Marco Travaglio, who's earned our admiration as a proud upholder of freedom of the press, is now sporting an IDF helmet and entertaining the masses on TV while amusing himself with the pastime most in vogue at the moment: infant-shooting in Gaza.

As I franticly tap at my keyboard in the Ramattan Press Agency office, all the Palestinian reporters around me are wearing bullet-proof vests and helmets. They haven't come in straight from driving a tank – they've simply been sitting in front of their computers the whole time. Two floors above, the Reuters offices were recently struck by a rocket, which seriously injured two. Almost all the floors in the building are empty at the moment, and only the most heroic of journalists are still around. The story of this hell must somehow continue to be told. And yet, earlier this week, the Israeli Army had assured Reuters it wouldn't need to evacuate, as they would be safe staying in their offices. This morning the bombing of the United Nations building also caused many casualties, built, among others, with money from the Italian government. Silvio Berlusconi, where are you?

John Ging, Director of UNRWA's Field Operations in Gaza, spoke frankly about white phosphorous bombs. In the Tal El-Hawa neighbourhood in Gaza City, a whole wing of Al-Quds Hospital is presently in flames. Leila, an ISM colleague is trapped inside, alongside 40 doctors and nurses and about 100 patients. She described these last dramatic hours to us by phone. A tank is stationed in front of the hospital. There are snipers everywhere, ready to shoot at anything. Destruction is all around. At night, from their windows, they could observe a building going up in flames after having been shelled. They heard the cries of whole families with children, pleading for help. They were impotent to help, watching people being devoured by flames, running out on to the street and then being reduced to ashes. Hell has switched places and come to the centre of Gaza, and we are the damned, designated as such by an inhuman hatred.

Stay human.

Subject: Turning Geography on its Head

Date: 16th January 2009

From: Vittorio Arrigoni

There's a story of an elderly Palestinian who leaves his house in search of his next meal during one of our rare morning ceasefires. But he is then unable to find his way back home. Shelling and bombing has radically changed Gaza's cityscape, warping its social structure with it as well. Hundreds of families are forced to flee to different destinations all over the whole of the Strip, and hundreds who used to live alongside one another before are now no longer even in touch. In order to reach the Tal El-Hawa neighbourhood in south-eastern Gaza City, you have to walk across a lunar landscape.

Leaving behind a trail of craters and mounds of rubble, the Israeli tanks yesterday have pulled away after a 48-hour siege. Ever-present in this desolate scenario is the lingering, pestilent and unmistakable stench of death. Struggling past what remains of entire buildings and houses, carcasses of burnt-out cars and ambulances, I started searching for Ahmed's house. It wasn't an easy task because of the radical transformation that whole neighbourhoods razed to the ground and burnt to cinders had endured at the hands of the Israeli military. I remembered that Ahmed lived at the end of a dirt road, impossible to recognize now that I was struggling to tread over one whole vast surface of debris that had been chewed and spat out by the tanks. If a satellite photo of Gaza were taken at the end of this massive genocidal attack, it would be difficult to convince anyone that the city in the photo was the same one pictured just 20 days earlier.

I had a chance to put my arms around Ahmed again – it was as if we hadn't seen one another in years after a long journey from somewhere far off. Unfortunately, our journey at the end of the night had no new dawn in sight, except the one set alight by the hatred of those ordering the generals and troops into action for this massacre. My friend showed me where an Israeli tank had stood for two days, right in front of his garden. During all that time his entire family had remained huddled underneath a stairwell, terrified that a shell shot by a howitzer might wipe them out at any minute. Only last night, Ahmed went against the orders of his apprehensive father and, dragging himself across the floor, dared to look out the window at the hellish scenario all around. He saw the tank moving about 30 metres away, smashing into the shutters of a supermarket and opening a hole in it. He then watched soldiers emerge from the armoured vehicle who cheerfully wandered in to 'do some shopping'. 'They filled the tank to the point that they were struggling to get back in.' He then described the jubilant laughs, the mocking songs, providing a soundtrack to the explosions all night long: 'Ali, Mohammed, this is a message to your Allah Akbar!'

The resistance, which for some days had stoically succeeded in limiting the advance of the Israeli tanks, fizzled out within a couple of hours. Kalashnikovs can only tickle plated tank armour, while the shells of howitzers can blow up a house from wall to wall. The residential neighbourhood of Abraj Towers, mainly inhabited by the families of the teaching staff from Al-Aqsa University and in large part sympathetic with Fatah, certainly does not host any 'Hamas terrorists'. The same way that I'm aware of this, I'm certain that it's also common knowledge in Tel Aviv. It didn't seem to matter, though, as the neighbourhood was reduced to a pile of rubble all the same.

Next to the crumbled buildings stands the Al-Quds Hospital, set on fire only yesterday. My ISM companions have assisted the hospital staff in evacuating the 300 wounded there to Gaza City's other hospital, Al-Shifa. It took them many hours, especially as moving seriously-injured patients required the use of specialist ambulances that the Palestinians don't have. We waited for the last evacuees with Dr Dagfinn Bjørklid from the Norwegian NGO NORWAC and asked some questions of the nurses who'd survived the Al-Quds fire.

These were blood-curdling stories, backed up by my companions' own eyewitness accounts. Around 200 metres from the hospital lay about 30 bodies, among them women and children, many of whom were still alive. They couldn't be rescued as the snipers on the roofs shot at anything that moved. Those bleeding bodies in the street were civilians who'd escaped from their homes when they'd caught fire after being shelled. The Israeli snipers hadn't hesitated to shoot them, one by one, including the children, once they were framed by the viewfinders on their guns.

I'll confess that my motto 'stay human' has been direly tested in the last few days, but has survived intact nevertheless. It pulled through, just as the pride for and attachment to one's native land, expressed as identity and the right to self-rule, has enabled Gaza's people to carry on. From the university professors to the people you meet in the street, doctors and nurses, reporters, fishermen, farmers, men, women and teenagers, those who've lost everything and those who had nothing to lose, all will use their last breath to say 'insha'Allah', for the sake of the sincere conviction that their roots run so deep that no enemy bulldozer can tear them out. As I write, a TV screen not far off is showing images from the inside of the Al-Shifa Hospital. Men in tears cover their faces as if to contain a flood of desperation. At Shija'iya, east of Gaza City, a shot from a tank just killed seven and wounded 25. The casualties were all at a funeral commemorating a family member who'd been killed the previous day. Yesterday the Israeli Defence Minister Ehud Barak apologized to the UN Secretary-General, Ban Ki-Moon, for the artillery fire against the UN Agency for Palestinian Refugees in Gaza City, which had been built with the Italian government's money. (Berlusconi, where are you?) 'It was a grave error', Barak said. There wasn't the trace of an apology to the families of the 357 Palestinian children killed up till now. Clearly, *that* was no error.

I listened a Red Cross paramedic tell me the story of their arrival on the scene of a massacre at Zeitoun. A visibly malnourished child crouched in front of his mother's corpse, already in an advanced state of decay. He had taken care of that body for four days, as if she were still alive. He had dried the blood from her face and dragging himself through the rubble of what had been their home, bringing her water, bread and tomatoes, which he'd carefully placed next to her head. He thought she was only sleeping.

The Israeli snipers had prevented the Red Cross from rushing in to bring aid, and they only managed to reach the scene of the massacre several days later.

Stay human.

Subject: Love under the Bombs

Date: 17th January 2009

From: Vittorio Arrigoni

Making love under the bombs. I remember a friend from Nablous once telling me how difficult it was during the occupation to reserve a moment of intimacy with his wife. One evening, while they lay in a tender embrace, a bullet lodged itself into their headboard, inches away from their heads. In Gaza these days canoodling under the bombs is out of the question, and the conjugal future of young Palestinian couples is shaping up to be quite a challenge. Many have lost their homes and are forced to live huddled together in the UNRWA schools, or crammed inside a tiny apartment with as many as 20 people. 'Tonight is Saturday and the young couples in Tel Aviv go out and have fun in the clubs or on the beach. Meanwhile, out here, we can't even make love in our own beds', says Wissam, who got married in November. 'We do have strobe lights though', he says, pointing to a succession of flashes to the south, the evidence of bombing in full swing. Young men like Wissam, himself aged nineteen, become fathers very early on in life and are already grandfathers by middle age, being aware that – as they are in Palestine – this is the only form of survival available to them.

While there's talk on the outside of a ceasefire, accepted by Hamas but, as usual, rejected by Israel, in the last two days there's been an escalation of bombings with a subsequent boost in civilian deaths – 60 only yesterday. About 10 were killed outside a mosque at the time of prayer. What worries Palestinians the most is the call for a ceasefire without reopening the border crossings at the same time. Even before materials for reconstruction are let in, food supplies are urgently needed, and those who've been seriously injured need to get out. Hospitals are overwhelmed from the overcrowding. In the entire Strip, they have a capacity of only 1,500 beds. But the number of the wounded presently hovers at around 5,320. In addition, Palestinian public opinion mistrusts Egypt, the chosen intermediary for the talks, whose leadership is notoriously obsequious to Israel. 'Why not have a European country mediate? The role of Germany, a truly neutral country, was decisive in the resolution of the conflict between Israel and Hizbullah,' says a heavy-hearted Hamza, a university professor.

This morning another UN school in Beit Lahiya, in the northern Gaza Strip, was heavily hit by Israeli tanks. There were 14 injured and two little brothers, Bilal and Mohammed Al-Ashqar, aged five and seven, were killed. Their mother survived, but lost both her legs. Along with 42,000 others, they had sought shelter in the school after Israel had ordered them to evacuate their homes. They believed they'd be safe there, just like the 43 refugees exterminated on the 6th January in the UNRWA school massacre in Jabilia. 'These two children were without a doubt innocent, just as there isn't the shadow of a doubt

30th December 2008: Mojma Al-Wezarat, Tal El-Hawa, Gaza City.
The ruins of bombed official government buildings
(Mohammed Al-Zaanoun and Majdi Fathi)

that they're now dead', said John Ging, the Director of
UNRWA's Field Operations in Gaza, who tirelessly, albeit
in vein, continues to report the war crimes committed
by the Israeli Army. But the Israeli generals are still busy
preparing the 'mission accomplished' speech they intend
to deliver to the world. I went back to what's left of Tal El-
Hawa Hospital, the part still standing after the building was
set on fire by the Israelis. It has now started operating as a
first aid unit and logistical base for ambulances again. They
continue to extract casualties trapped for days under the
rubble, found around its seriously-damaged buildings. Al-
Shifa Hospital hosts a child called Suhaib Suliman, the only
survivor in a family of 25, all of whom are dead. A young

girl, Hadil Samony, lost 11 relatives. She'll have no one to take care of her after being discharged from hospital.

Excuse me, but can someone please explain what kind of mission this is? It's straight from collective punishment to mass slaughter. On his blog, a frustrated Arab called Raja Chemayel sums it all up as follows:

Take a strip of land about 40 km long and only five km wide. Call it Gaza. Then cram in 1.4 million inhabitants. After that surround it by the sea to the west, Egypt with Mubarak in the south, Israel in the north, and dub it 'The land of terrorists'. After that, declare war against it and invade it with 232 tanks, 687 armoured vehicles, 43 airports for fighter jets, 105 war helicopters, 221 units of ground artillery, 349 mortars, three spy satellites, 64 informers, 12 spies and 8,000 assault troops. Then call all of this 'Israel defending itself'. After that, stop for a minute and state that you will 'avoid hitting the civilian population' and call yourself the only democracy in action. Whichever way you look at it, only a miracle could prevent you hitting those civilians, or it could quite simply be a lie. But once again, just call it 'Israel defending itself'. Now comes the question: what would happen if the invader turned out to be a liar? What would happen to those unarmed civilians? With such firepower, how could even Mother Theresa, or Mickey Mouse, avoid hitting all those civilians, considering the ... situation? Call it whatever you like, but Israel knew damn well those unarmed people were out there. It was Israel itself that had put them there. So, go ahead and call it genocide. It's much more credible.

Aside from a couple of brutally-assassinated leaders, Hamas hasn't suffered from this attack, and certainly hasn't lost its popularity. If anything, they've gained some more. Once in a while it would be wise to remember that Hamas aren't a bunch of terrorists, nor a political party, but a movement, and as such they're impossible to neutralize with storms of cluster bombs.

When I ask Palestinians for their opinions on the real agenda behind this brutal massacre, many say it has everything to do with the Israeli elections in February.[5] They made successful propaganda, one vote at a time. It's always been like this on the eve of all elections. Just a month ago, Benjamin Netanyahu was forecast to be the sure winner, but he's now expected to lose in competing against the bloodthirsty vision of Ehud Olmert and Tzipi Livni. Avigdor Lieberman is the leader of Yisrael Beitenu, a growing political force, that had won 11 seats after the 2006 elections, but the polls show that they are gaining in popularity even while alluding to the use of a nuclear option against Hamas as the Americans did against the Japanese at the end of World War Two.[6] Yesterday Israeli writer Abraham Yehoshua stated to *Haaretz*: 'We kill their children today to save many more tomorrow.' I'm afraid

---

5. The Israeli elections, held on the 10th February 2009, were narrowly won by the centrist party Kadima, led by Tzipi Livni, but as Kadima were unable to form a viable coalition, its right-wing rival, Likud, led by Benjamin Netanyahu, went on to lead a successful alliance into power.

6. In the 2009 elections, Yisrael Beitenu became the third largest party with 15 seats and joined the Likud party to from the next government. See the full quote from Lieberman on p. 114.

that now, his 'Journey to the End of the Millennium' has ended up on board a tank in front of a hospital in flames. Voltaire invited us to respect all opinions. I would suggest stopping the sowing of seeds of hatred, sprinkling them with blood and feeding them with terminal resentment.

Stay human.

Subject: The Living and the Dead

Date: 19th January 2009

From: Vittorio Arrigoni

In Gaza, only the dead have seen the end of war. For the living, no ceasefire can make up for the daily battle of a constant quest for survival. They have no running water, gas, electricity, and no bread and milk with which to feed their children. Thousands of people have lost their homes. Humanitarian aid seeps through the passes in dribs and drabs, and you get the feeling that the benevolence of the killers' accomplices is only temporary. Tomorrow, Ban Ki-Moon, the UN's Secretary General, will travel to Gaza, and we're pretty sure that John Ging, Director of UNRWA's Field Operations in Gaza, will have many stories to tell him after Israel bombed two UN schools, assassinated four of their workers, and bombed and destroyed the UNRWA Centre in Gaza City, reducing tonnes of medicine and food supplies destined for the civilian population to ashes in the process.

Gaza's mountains of rubble continue to spit corpses back out on to the surface. Yesterday in Jabalia, Tal El-Hawa in Gaza City and Zeitoun, the Red Crescent paramedics, with some help from the ISM volunteers, have pulled out a total of 95 corpses from the ruins, many of which are in an advanced state of decay. Walking through the streets of the city and no longer feeling constantly terrified by the thought of a bomb surgically aimed to decapitate me, I still tremble at the sight of stray dogs gathering in a circle, imagining what could reveal itself before my eyes as constituting their meal. Relieved-looking men go back to hanging out in their mosques and cafés, but their attitude of feigned normalcy is easy to detect. Many of them have lost a relative or have nowhere to live. They pretend to go back to their everyday routine to boost their wives and children's morale – somehow, even this catastrophe must be dealt with.

This morning we drove in some ambulances to the most devastated neighbourhoods in the city, Tal el-Hawa and Zeitoun. Questionnaire in hand, we went door-to-door compiling a survey of the extent of the damage to the buildings, and wrote down the families' most urgent requirements: medicine for the sick and elderly, and rice, oil and flour – basically the essentials – to feed themselves with. All that we've been able to give them so far are metres of nylon, to be used in lieu of their shattered windowpanes to block out the cold. ISM colleagues in Rafah informed me that the municipality has handed out a few thousand dollars – mere pennies – to the families who've had their houses completely razed to the ground by the bombs, the very same that according to Israel, had only been dropped to destroy the tunnels. After the end of the conflict with Lebanon, Hizbullah had donated millions of dollars in cheques to support homeless Lebanese citizens. In Gaza, embargoed and under siege, Hamas is hardly able to support its people with what 'would barely be enough to rebuild a barn for livestock', says Khaled, a Rafah farmer.

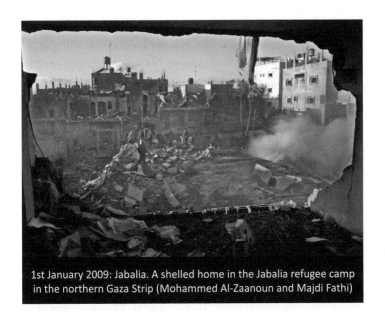

1st January 2009: Jabalia. A shelled home in the Jabalia refugee camp in the northern Gaza Strip (Mohammed Al-Zaanoun and Majdi Fathi)

As the truce is unilateral, Israel unilaterally decides not to respect it. In Khan Yunis, a Palestinian boy was killed yesterday, and another was injured. East of Gaza City, helicopters have showered a residential area with white phosphorous. The same happened in Jabalia. In Khan Yunis today, the warships shot their cannons at an open plain, thankfully without harming anyone. But, as I write, news of advancing tanks has reached me. We're not aware of any Palestinian rockets having been fired in the past 24 hours.

International journalists are clamouring for news all along the Strip. They only managed to get in today. Israel granted them a pass only now that the massacre is winding down. Those who got here in the thick of the battle braved deadly risks, as I was told by Lorenzo Cremonesi, a correspondent for Italian daily *Corriere della Sera*. Israeli soldiers shot bullet holes into the car he was travelling in. Standing by the blackened skeleton of what remains of Al-Quds Hospital in Gaza City, an astonished BBC reporter asked me how the army could possibly have mistaken the building for a terrorists' den. I said: 'For the very same reason that children running away from burning buildings are put in the sights of snipers on the roofs, who then don't hesitate to kill them, spreading their grey matter all over the road.' The journalist furrowed his brow further. The enormous difference between us eyewitnesses and firsthand victims of the massacre, and those who heard about it through our stories, is now further highlighted.

From Rome I'm told that the EU intends to freeze the funds assigned for the reconstruction of Gaza while it's still being governed by Hamas. The European Commissioner for External Relations, Benita Ferrero-Waldner, has made her point clear on this score: 'The aid for the reconstruction of the Strip', stated the European diplomat, 'will only arrive if Palestinian President Abu Mazen will once again re-establish his authority over the territory.' For Gaza's Palestinians this is an explicit invitation from the outside to engage in civil war, or in a *coup d'état*. It's equivalent to legitimizing the massacre of 410 children, who died because their parents support democracy and freely elected Hamas.

'The EU is diligently echoing the criminal policy of collective punishment imposed by Israel. Why not entrust the funds to the UN? Or some governmental organization? The Unites States are free to elect a warmonger like Bush, Israel can choose leaders with bloodied hands like Sharon or Netanyahu, but we, the people of Gaza, aren't free to chose Hamas?', suggested Mohamed, a human rights activist, who had never voted for the Islamic movement. I had no arguments to contradict him.

Living Palestinians learn from their dead; they learn to live while dying, right from the youngest age. Truce after truce, the general perception here is that of a macabre pause during which to count the dead between one massacre and another, and peace has never felt so elusive. Scouring Gaza City on board an ambulance with the siren switched off for once, the war is still everywhere, among the ruins of a city pillaged of smiles and now populated only by frightened gazes, eyes that insist upon scanning the sky for the planes still flying endlessly overhead.

Inside a home we visited with some paramedics, I noticed some pastel drawings on the floor. It was clearly a child's hand that had abandoned them after evacuating the house in a mad rush. I picked one of them up – tanks, helicopters and a body in pieces. In the middle of the drawing a child with a stone had succeeded in reaching the sun's height and was damaging one of the flying death machines. It's been said that in a child's drawing, the sun represents their desire to be, to exist. The sun I saw was crying tears of blood coloured in red pastel. Is a unilateral ceasefire enough to heal such traumas?

Stay human.

Subject: Traces of Death

Date: 20th January 2009

From: Vittorio Arrigoni

'When the details of Gaza's massive destruction become known, my only reason to travel to Amsterdam will be to appear before The Hague's International Court.' These words were ascribed by the *Haaretz* newspaper to an Israeli minister, who prefers to remain anonymous.

All around the world, indignant humanitarian organizations and citizens wish to see the Israeli Army and its government dragged into the courtroom, hoping they'll be found guilty of the war crimes their hands were bloodied with during the 22-day massacre in Gaza.

In their public appearances, the military and government leaderships don't seem too phased. They claim to have solid proof that the sites they bombed were all support bases used by Hamas terrorists. Let me get this straight: we're talking about thousands of houses damaged by the shelling, including 1,300 human casualties.

To check out these alleged, crucial strategic hide-outs of Islamic terrorism, I headed to one of the most heavily bombed areas, Jabal Al-Dardour in the northern Strip. Dozens of buildings had been razed to the ground. The mammoth-sized, armour-plated bulldozers are custom-built by Caterpillar (boycott it!) to raze Palestinian houses to the ground, and are used to lend the army tanks a hand in their destructive effort. Out there I saw men and women rummaging through the rubble, looking for things, such as an article of clothing, a few dust-coated school bags or portrait photos of families in cracked frames. I've never caught sight of any destroyed arsenals, only buildings with their ceilings torn clear off their walls, where you can catch sight of what was once a living-room, the remains of a bedroom, or a kitchen reduced to cinders.

Abu Omar, a molecular biologist, has invited me to come and see what's left of his apartment. His neighbour, Osama, a paediatrician, also showed me his house, reduced to a colander. The propulsive power of the missiles splashed some debris from the near-by orange orchard onto the building. The juice of oranges, mixed with the clotted blood splattered all over the floor, looked like a naïf painter's canvas.

An elderly man, his head wrapped in a kafiyeh, approaches us to ask Natalie, our Lebanese companion with the ISM, where she's from. Waving his walking stick in the air, as if to draw a wide arc over the devastated landscape before us, he says, 'Beirut and Gaza, same painting, same artist.' Even Osama's pigeon coop hasn't been spared by the shelling. His birds lie on the ground, as if defeated by a sky too heavy for their wings, as heavy as 'cast lead'. 'They tried to defeat the Palestinian air force, or perhaps they thought these birds might be dispatch carriers for Hamas', I told the paediatrician, causing him to smile sadly.

As we travelled in our broken-down taxi, we crossed routes with the UN's Secretary-General, Ban Ki-Moon. A long line of brand-new SUVs, all tinted windows and UN logos, darted through Gaza as if the earth shook beneath their tires. As it happens, this was actually the case until a few days ago.

Wandering around the impossible puzzle of Jabal Al-Dardour's ruins, I heard someone call my name. When I looked over my shoulder, I saw Abu Ashrafa. I'd attended his son's funeral when he was killed by a bomb last November, a month in which – according to Israel and the Western media – a ceasefire had been called. Abu Ashrafa had just lost another relative, and his house has been razed down to its foundations. 'They haven't left us a single head of livestock, a rock, or an olive tree standing – they're not human', he said, leading me to his olive orchard.

Many trees – the centenary ones – have been torn down by Israeli bulldozers. It's as if they were trying to make up for not being able to erase lives that are impossible to uproot from their origins, their identity and their burning desire for justice, surviving all destruction. Not far away a middle-aged man approached me, asking if I thought all Palestinians were Hamas guerrilla fighters. From a window in his damaged home flapped a yellow Fatah banner. 'Our Kalashnikov is our faith and honour, we will stand up for our land tooth and nail in the same way you would defend your daughter from being raped', this Fatah supporter told me.

If Israel's objective was to isolate and rid the Strip of Hamas by dividing further a people already split by internal diatribes, then Israel has achieved the exact opposite of what it intended. The bombing has in part given Gaza back its national identity. The litmus test of this new situation is represented by the *muqawama*, the Palestinian resistance, heroic in its attempt to stop the Israeli Army from advancing. The flowing beards of the Izz Al-Din Al-Qassam Brigades'

Islamists, Hamas' fighting wing, have fought side-by-side with the scampish, goatee-sporting Marxist guerrilla fighters of the Popular Front for the Liberation of Palestine, and alongside Fatah's Al-Aqsa Martyrs Brigades. Only time will tell if this newfound unity among the militias is a reflection of unity within civic and political society.

Leaving the lunar atmosphere of Jabal Al-Dardour behind us, denuded of its buildings, we paused before a frowning child sitting atop a small pile of rubble, or what was left of his house's courtyard. We asked him what was going through his mind. In his simple words he seemed to be saying that Hamas and its resistance were responsible for this catastrophe. So Fida, our ISM companion took him aside in a motherly manner and briefly told him of their history. She spoke of soldiers marching into Rafah in 2004 and razing entire neighbourhoods to the ground, exactly as had happened here and now. Back then, there was no Hamas, and Fatah's leader, Yasser Arafat, was the designated terrorist, the number one enemy to dethrone and wipe away from Palestine. But rather than targeting Fatah's headquarters, even then the Israeli troops struck indiscriminately and killed dozens of civilians, razing Fida's house in the process as well.

Travelling back towards Gaza City, the car in which we drove plunged into a hole in the concrete created by the tanks' creaking wheels. The taxi driver turned around and said: 'Death was here and left its footprints.' I wonder how long it'll take for the scars of this land to heal.

Stay human.

I crossed the threshold of my house in Almina, facing Gaza City's port, after several days' absence. Everything was exactly as I had left it – the gas tank was still anorexic (feeding it is too expensive) and the power had been cut off by a perfect stranger's pliers. The pleasant panorama that had once been outside my window has changed and no longer raises my spirits from the miseries of living under siege. To the contrary, it now rubs salt in the wound, a trauma that won't heal with its reminders of a massacre. Twenty metres from my front door, where the fire station once stood, a huge crater now gapes wide for children to mess around in, as if to exorcize its horror for their parents.

The afternoon call to prayer no longer has the same comforting quality of the muezzin's chant that I had grown accustomed to. I wonder where he's gone to, and if he managed to survive at the top of one of the few minarets still left intact. The last time I'd listened to him, this anonymous muezzin had had to interrupt his solemnly chanted call to prayer because of a chesty cough. It's an affliction I'm familiar with myself, as the gases of the bombing in Gaza have spared no one. I found a note at the foot of the French window looking onto my small balcony, as if it had been put there by a friend. The street and garden were littered with these same leaflets. They had been dropped from Israeli airplanes warning the Palestinians to stay alert, and be aware that the walls had ears and eyes. 'At the slightest threatening action against Israel we'll be back to invade the Gaza Strip again. What you've seen these days is nothing compared with what awaits you.' Some kids in the streets had picked up the leaflets and folded them into paper airplanes, seemingly sending the message back to its destination.

Over the phone, Ahmed told me about a new kids' game. Until a few days ago, they amused themselves by relighting the fires, simply kicking the fragments of white phosphorous bombs found scattered all over the Strip. The debris left by these bombs has very long-lasting flammable properties. Even when picked up several days after their detonation, they can still catch fire if shaken about. The Al-Quds Hospital paramedics speak of how they have given up trying to put out the fires provoked by these illegal bombs – their flames seemed to feed off the water being thrown at them. 'The consequences of all the sh*t that's been thrown at us in these last three weeks will surface again in the near future, with new cancer cases and deformed babies', Munir, a doctor at Al-Shifa Hospital told me.

Even Gaza's neighbours seem to be worrying about this massive use of weapons forbidden by all international conventions. In Sderot, and likewise in Ashkelon, Israeli citizens have formally asked their government for clarification regarding the weapons that have been used to torment us. It's obvious that impoverished uranium and white phosphorous scattered in such a criminal manner all over the tiny patch of land that is Gaza won't discriminate between Jews and Muslims when it comes to provoking generic illnesses.

The truce ought to have started by now, but today I was awoken in my bed by the deafening rumble of cannon fire from the warships, exactly like a few days ago. Some brave Palestinian fishermen had ventured from the port equipped with fishing nets on their tiny boats. The Israeli Navy pushed them back. Nowadays, the only edible fish found in Gaza are the Egyptian cans of tuna that came through the tunnels months ago. East of Gaza City two children were blown up when playing with an unexploded device. The witnesses we met spoke of active mines in front of the ruins of Tal El-Hawa's houses. Some bomb disposal experts sent over by Hamas defused them and, judging by the care with which they loaded them onto an off-road vehicle, I think the Izz Al-Din Al-Qassam Brigades might return those messages of death straight back to their lawful owners sometime soon.

Looking from Naeema's roof, the Israeli-Palestinian border has never seemed so easy to pick out. On one side lie green hills, being constantly watered by the Israeli kibbutzim. On the other you see the parching thirst of a land robbed of its water springs and herds. Naeema wished to tell me all about her last few days – a tactile, aural and olfactory account of the massacre, considering that young Naeema is blind. The soldiers threateningly ordered her fellow villagers to evacuate their homes only a few minutes before storming the place. The men loaded the younger children onto their shoulders and ran away, along with their women. Naeema chose to stay so as not to slow down their escape. She took refuge in her own home, believing herself to be safe, and welcomed her neighbours, who had nowhere else to go: three women, an elderly lady and a paralyzed old man.

Then the tanks and bulldozers came, spreading death and destruction, devouring acre upon acre, until they stopped in front of Naeema's house. Standing on a small hill, the building she inhabits is the tallest in the village, and the Israeli soldiers, who found that it was strategically positioned, let themselves in and occupied it for two weeks. 'They came in and pointed their weapons at us, pushing us into a small room, where they locked us up for 11 days', Naeema said. 'During that entire time they only brought us water to drink twice, and food came in the form of leftovers from the soldiers' rations. They never let us go to the bathroom, so we had to relieve ourselves in one corner of the room. They wouldn't let us talk among ourselves, and would come in and beat us at night, when, huddled in a circle, we tried to gather some strength from prayer. Sometimes they'd come over and, intimidating us by pressing their weapons against our napes, they demanded that we confess our alleged support for Hamas, insulting us when we wouldn't comply.'

At the end of the eleventh day of imprisonment, the International Red Cross finally arrived and released the six prisoners from their jailers. 'They didn't allow us to pick anything up, not even my sunglasses', Naeema related, bringing her story to a close, adding that when she and her neighbours returned to their homes, they discovered the thievery carried out by the soldiers. They had taken all their gold trinkets and hidden savings, after having destroyed their few possessions: two TV sets, a radio, a fridge, and the solar panels on the roofs. I saw tears in this woman's eyes, hidden by her dark glasses. They seemed the most vivid I had ever seen. In actual fact, what Naeema 'saw' is a lot more that any young woman her age will ever get a chance to see, if she had the misfortune of being born in this tortured strip of land.

Stay human.

Subject: The Epicentre of the Catastrophe Continues

Date: 29th July 2009

From: Vittorio Arrigoni

The siege is the core of nothingness. It's the centre of human misery. It's the centre of desperation and a growing sense of faltering hope.

John Ging, Director of Field Operations in Gaza, United Nations Relief and Works Agency for Palestine Refugees

Six months after the end of the Israeli offensive known as 'Cast Lead', the Gaza Strip still seems a violated land, the very epicentre of a recent and violent earthquake.

Nothing much has changed since the 18th January, the last day of the bombing campaign. Its gaping wounds are still visible today: the Strip is still in large part reduced to rubble. The much-discussed reconstruction plans remain on paper. Action has been limited to distributing handfuls of dollars to move the rubble from one place to another. The persistent blockade of the borders imposed by Tel Aviv on land, sea and air has prevented most aid from reaching Gaza. According to a report by the UN Office for the Coordination of Humanitarian Affairs (OCHA), the ban on imported materials for reconstruction, on spare parts for machinery, and even on financial transactions has prevented any reconstruction on almost all planned projects. During the massacre, 21,000 civilian buildings were destroyed or damaged by Israeli shelling, including 57 medical centres, 51 schools and 59 UN schools, in addition to 1,500 factories and shops, 20 water and sewage networks and power plants, the cost of repairing the damage and destruction has been estimated at 1.9 billion dollars in value.

One hundred thousand Palestinians became homeless from one day to the next, many of whom are forced to live in tents in the refugee camps at Zeitoun and Abed Rabbo. This traumatic tragedy has once again evoked the memory of the Nakba, the Palestinian catastrophe of 1948. Back then, following a systematic policy of ethnic cleansing from Israel, hundreds of thousands of Palestinians were chased off their lands and were forced to keep alive what slender hopes for a new life they might have still entertained in the refugee camps.

Reconstruction is simply not happening now because the ban on cement and other building materials is still firmly in place. Not even piping or other spare parts for the water and sewage networks can get an Israeli stamp of approval, forcing over 250,000 people to live without running water, while 40% of the population have no electricity because electrical wires and other spare parts are also forbidden.

Israel claims that it has placed a ban on concrete because Palestinians would use it to rebuild the tunnels at Rafah. Yet the tunnels represent the only available form of relief when it comes to procuring rations and essential goods for the civilian population, trapped now for over two years in the grip of a ruthless siege. Israel won't allow iron in either, because the armed groups would construct the infamous, homemade Qassam 'rockets' with the metal. Israel even prevents the entry of glass, but what their excuse for this is, I don't know. When you visit the main hospitals along the Strip, looking at the facades of the buildings, you can still easily pick out the nylon sheets stretched over the windows to replace the glass panes shattered by the bombs.

Besides material for reconstruction, Israel is denying entry to an endless list of products for everyday use. In total, only 40 commercial goods are allowed into the Strip, compared with about 4,000 that were approved before the start of the siege. Every week, 10 Israeli Army officers hold a COGAT meeting (Coordination of Government Activities in the Territories) and decide what types of food and which goods may be let through to support the survival of 1.5 million Palestinians. The few goods that have free access are subdivided into three categories: food, medicine and detergents. Everything else is banned: building and plumbing materials, machinery and spare parts for cars, textile goods, threads, needles, light bulbs, candles, matches, musical instruments, books, clothes, shoes, mattresses, bed linen, blankets, cutlery, crockery, cups, glasses and livestock. Recently, Colonels Moshe Levi, Alex Rosenzweig and Doron Segal, chief executors at COGAT, have become more lenient towards fruits and vegetables such as bananas, khaki fruit, apples, pumpkins and carrots. Meanwhile apricots, prunes and avocados arbitrarily continue to be considered luxury items. For some time now, the Palestinian population have been allowed access to melons, a decision taken by the economic division of COGAT, on the basis of wanting to prevent its sales plummeting in Israel. Access to delights such as cherries, kiwi fruits, almonds, pomegranates and chocolate are strictly forbidden. The decision regarding which products should be classified as 'luxury items' changes from one week to the next, and sometimes daily. Pasta, which was banned in the past, is now allowed in, thanks to US Senator John Kerry's intervention. He came on a visit to Gaza last February and was stunned to hear of the pasta ban. Pasta can now be found on the shelves of food stores that don't stock frozen goods, tinned meats, 160 types of medicine, tea, coffee, semolina, cured meats and dairy products. Only a very limited amount of industrial fuel is allowed, which is the reason why the power plants are often short of fuel, causing daily blackouts in random areas of the Gaza Strip.

While the changeover of Israeli ministers and leaders was taking place, Israel announced to the world that no humanitarian crisis currently exists in Gaza. They won't shy away from highlighting the hundreds of trucks that enter the Strip through Israeli borders, but it's really too bad that the UN has specified that at least 500 truckloads of aid a day would be necessary to cover only a small part of the civilian population's basic needs under the current siege conditions. According to UNICEF, since the Israeli offensive, the situation in Gaza has, predictably enough, worsened considerably. Before Operation 'Cast Lead', 80% of the Strip's population relied on humanitarian aid. After a military campaign of just 22 days, that percentage rose to 88%. In street corners, a growing number of children beg for a few coins from passing cars, while selling bunches of parsley and mint, their faces dirty and their clothes tattered. I wonder what has happened to their families.

As a left-wing Italian, it was a paradox for me to demonstrate alongside the Palestinian Communist groups on May Day, celebrating workers in a land where the rate of unemployment is now well over 70%. After January, the siege conditions haven't just tightened for the movement of primary goods into the Strip, but also for the freedom of movement of its inhabitants. The Rafah Pass, on the border with Egypt, opens its gates for just a couple of days a month. Among the thousands of Palestinians with regular passports and visas for Europe or America crowding the border and hoping each time to make a breakthrough, only a few hundred manage to get a chance to breathe some fresher air outside this huge open-air prison.

It's worth remembering that from June 2007 to July 2009, 346 people have died from a lack of adequate medical care within the Gaza Strip. These very sick people had official papers to request access to better-equipped hospitals in the West, but Israel, with Egyptian complicity, has sentenced them to death, as they waited in vain behind sealed borders. The living and the dead are condemned for the sole sin of having chosen a government through free and democratic elections, and for not having succumbed to their armed oppressors.

Stay human.

Subject: War Crimes in Gaza

Date: 3rd August 2009

From: Vittorio Arrigoni

> We train young men to drop fire on people. But their commanders won't allow them to write 'f*ck' on their airplanes because it's obscene!
>
> **Colonel Kurtz – *Apocalypse Now***

The Israeli Army has acquitted itself of any misdeeds after having submitted itself to five internal 'investigations'. Here are the conclusions they have come to: 'Throughout the fighting in Gaza the IDF operated in accordance with international law.' The killings of unarmed civilians have been defined as 'intelligence or operational errors'. Amnesty International has dismissed these claims for lack of credibility. Israel had failed 'to properly investigate its forces' conduct in Gaza, including war crimes' and refused to cooperate with the UN's independent fact-finding mission.

In its July report, *Operation Cast Lead*, Amnesty accused Israel of having committed 'war crimes' from the moment that it used 'battlefield weapons against a civilian population trapped in Gaza, with no means of escape.'[7] The report reveals that the magnitude and intensity of the attacks on Gaza are 'unprecedented'. They confirm the statistics of the Hamas government's Ministry of Health, reporting that 'some 300 children and hundreds of other unarmed civilians who took no part in the conflict were among the 1,400 Palestinians killed by Israeli forces.' Amnesty found that:

> victims of the attacks it investigated were not caught in the crossfire during battles between Palestinian militants and Israeli forces, nor were they shielding militants or other military objects. Many were killed when their homes were bombed while they slept. Other were sitting in their yard or hanging the laundry on the roof. Children were struck while playing in their bedrooms or on the roof, or near their homes. Paramedics and ambulances were repeatedly attacked while attempting to rescue the wounded or recover the dead.

Amnesty's investigators discovered that the majority of casualties were killed by 'high-precision weapons, relying on surveillance drones that have exceptionally good optics, allowing those observing to see their targets in detail', thus discrediting the Israeli government's claims that civilian deaths were a result of 'collateral damage'.

The report also condemned the use of white phosphorous, which unlike the other weapons is dubbed

---

7. Amnesty International, *Operation Cast Lead: 22 Days of Death and Destruction* (London: Amnesty International, July 2009).

'imprecise', and 'never to be used in densely populated areas', such as the Gaza Strip, with its 3,945.4 people per square kilometre – making it one of the most heavily populated areas on the planet.

Before Amnesty's intervention, it was a report, *Rain of Fire*, published by Human Rights Watch, that first highlighted Israel's war crimes.[8] Once again, it was the use of white phosphorous weapons that was most emphasised. The NGO maintained that the Israeli Army was well aware of the substance's lethal potential to burn anything it comes in contact with until it has totally burnt itself out. In living organisms it can inflict serious damage to the internal organs. When shot, phosphorous bombs, also known as M825 155mm smoke projectiles, shoot out 116 fragments of incandescent phosphorous, that can reach a radius of 125 metres. 'The repeated use of air-burst white phosphorous in populated areas', reports Human Rights Watch, 'reveals a pattern or policy of conduct rather than incidental or accidental usage.' According to military manuals, white phosphorous ammunitions are used to create smokescreens behind which soldiers can move on the ground without being seen. However, the report documented cases 'where the military value of white phosphorus fired as an apparent obscurant appeared to be minimal given the absence of Israeli forces in the vicinity. By comparison, the expected harm to civilians and civilian objects by using white phosphorus was often high, and thus disproportionate in violation of the laws of war.'

---

8. Human Rights Watch, *Rain of Fire: Israel's Unlawful Use of White Phosphorous* (New York: Human Rights Watch, March 2009).

During the massacre, it's worth remembering that the International Red Cross also raised its voice in condemnation of the human rights violations against wounded Palestinians and medical staff. Even within Israel, the humanitarian organization, Physicians for Human Rights (PHR), has charged Cast Lead with 'violations of the international humanitarian law and the Israeli army's ethical code ... [with respect to] medical personnel, damage to medical facilities and indiscriminate attacks on civilians not involved in the fighting.' The Israeli Army, concludes the PHR report, *Ill Morals*, 'impeded emergency medical evacuation of the sick and wounded declined ..., to help evacuate injured civilians and trapped families, ... [and] soldiers acted in [a] trigger-happy manner as they opened fire on ambulances, medical installations, and medical personnel.'[9] Specifically, 16 Palestinian medical personnel have been killed in combat and a further 25 were injured when they came to the aid of civilians.

Despite the fact that Defence Minister Ehud Barak continues to dub the Israeli Army 'the most moral in the world', Israel has refused to cooperate with the investigation set in place by the UN Council for Human Rights, led by Richard Goldstone. The latter clearly specified that he intended to investigate violations of international human rights laws committed by all those involved in the conflict that unfolded in Gaza and southern Israel. Israel's refusal to take part should not surprise one so much, since only a real democracy puts its army on trial for war crimes.

---

9. Dan Magen, *'Ill Morals': Grave Violations of the Right to Health during the Israeli Assault on Gaza* (Tel Aviv: Physicians for Human Rights, March 2009).

Israel has repeatedly demonstrated that it is not as yet a fully-fledged democracy.[10]

The Adiv fabric-printing shop in south Tel Aviv is busy selling T-shirts to soldiers with catchphrases such as 'Better use Durex', featuring a picture of a murdered Palestinian child and a mother crying over its body, or the logo 'One shot, two kills', accompanied by the picture of a pregnant Palestinian woman seen through a gun's viewfinder.[11] Meanwhile, eyewitness accounts of Israeli soldiers involved in Operation Cast Lead are now impacting upon public opinion. Blood-curdling stories, dozens of them, told by the pupils of the Yitzhak Rabin pre-military academy, give a sense of the Israeli Army's 'high morality':

> 'There was a house with a family inside .... We put them in a room. Later we left the house and another platoon entered it, and a few days after that there was an order to release the family. They had set up positions upstairs. There was a sniper position on the roof,' the soldier said.

> 'The platoon commander let the family go and told them to go to the right. One mother and her two children didn't understand and went to the left, but they forgot to tell the sharpshooter on the roof they had let them go and it was okay, and he should hold his fire and he ... he did what he was supposed to, like he was following his orders.'

10. The report released in September 2009 was heavily critical of Israel, finding that Operation Cast Lead was a 'deliberately disproportionate attack' and that there had been grave breaches of the Geneva Conventions, involving 'individual criminal responsibility'.

11. Uri Blau, 'Dead Palestinian babies and bombed mosques - IDF fashion 2009', *Haaretz*, 18th August 2009.

According to the squad leader: 'The sharpshooter saw a woman and children approaching him, closer than the lines he was told no one should pass. He shot them straight away. In any case, what happened is that in the end he killed them.

'I don't think he felt too bad about it, because after all, as far as he was concerned, he did his job according to the orders he was given. And the atmosphere in general, from what I understood from most of my men who I talked to ... I don't know how to describe it .... The lives of Palestinians, let's say, is something very, very less important than the lives of our soldiers. So as far as they are concerned they can justify it that way,' he said.

Another squad leader from the same brigade told of an incident where the company commander ordered that an elderly Palestinian woman be shot and killed; she was walking on a road about 100 meters from a house the company had commandeered.

The squad leader said he argued with his commander over the permissive rules of engagement that allowed the clearing out of houses by shooting without warning the residents beforehand. After the orders were changed, the squad leader's soldiers complained that 'we should kill everyone there [in the centre of Gaza]. Everyone there is a terrorist.'[12]

---

12. Amos Harel, 'IDF in Gaza: Killing civilians, vandalism, and lax rules of engagement', *Haaretz*, 19th March 2009.

The rules were, so to speak, fairly flexible in their application, and fuelled by unrelenting hatred, a worship of military superiority, and the prejudice that all Palestinians are terrorists.

Aside from cases of shooting civilians without warning against civilians, a commander describes episodes of vandalism in Palestinian homes: 'To write "death to the Arabs" on the walls, to take family pictures and spit on them, just because you can. I think this is the main thing: To understand how much the IDF has fallen in the realm of ethics, really. It's what I'll remember the most.'[13]

The Israeli government turned a blind eye to the controversy caused by these testimonies, speaking of a few 'black sheep' in a field full of innocent white lambs. It's the same old search for a scapegoat. From Guantánamo to Abu Ghraib, the search ends in the fenced-off rubble of Gaza City.

Stay human.

---

13. Amos Harel, 'Shooting and Crying', *Haaretz*, 20th March 2009.

Subject: Let them come to Gaza

Date: 19th August 2009

From: Vittorio Arrigoni

> *Tolerance becomes a crime when it is applied to evil.*
> **Thomas Mann**

Gaza's muted Palestinians survive while others speak for them while they may not speak for themselves. The pen dipped in blood that traces their destinies is held by a distant and bitter enemy, who decides the timing of the agony of a million-and-a-half people, depending on which way the pendulum of an uncaring electorate will swing.

Even toddlers around here know that the last massacre was a carnage promoted mainly for electoral purposes. More than 1,400 dead, 85% of whom were civilians, have provoked an amazing surge in approval for Ehud Olmert and Tzipi Livni, although that was not enough to allow them to beat Benjamin Netanyahu, a man with a turret for a head and tank treads for feet. From the start, the agenda of Netanyahu's government has been explicit and crystal clear: extending the colonies in the West Bank, and engaging in an open and endless war against Hamas. To the shock of Western diplomats, the delicate role of Foreign

Minister was assigned to Avigdor Lieberman, leader of Yisrael Beitenu ('Israel is our motherland'). No representing the third largest political force in the Knesset, the Israeli Parliament, during the election campaign Lieberman, in the run-up to the February 2009 elections, made the horrifying argument that an atomic bomb should be dropped on Gaza. During Operation 'Cast Lead', he argued that, 'We must continue to fight Hamas just like the United States did with the Japanese in World War II',[14] which was interpreted by many as alluding to the dropping of nuclear bombs on Hiroshima and Nagasaki in 1945 by the Americans in order to force an end to the Second World War. In his first speech as Foreign Minister in April, Lieberman clarified his vision of *shalom*, of *salama*, of enduring peace: '"*Si vis pacem, para bellum*" – if you want peace, prepare for war; be strong.' One could die in Gaza searching for a more explicit way of dressing up 'might is right' as 'peace'.

Western political leaders continue to engage in pleasant diplomatic relations with characters of the ilk of Olmert, Livni, Barak, Netanyahu, and Lieberman, whom it would be quite right to prosecute in any international court for violations of international law. On the other hand, no one must speak to Hamas – they must be embargoed, and, along with them, 1.5 million Palestinians must also be punished for freely voting for them in democratic elections. My International Solidarity Movement companions and I continue our actions of non-violent, civil protest, in support

---

14. Associated Free Press, 'Treat Hamas like Japan in WWII: Israeli nationalist leader', 13th January 2009.

of a civilian population strangled by a criminal siege. Meanwhile, Israel tells the world of a truce that doesn't exist: in Gaza, 'Operation Cast Lead' continues at regular intervals in all but name.

The tunnels at Rafah continue to be sporadically bombed, burying Palestinian miners when they collapse. Snipers take potshots at farmers working their lands along the borders. After the bombing, Israel announced that a corridor one kilometre beyond its borders with the Gaza Strip, in other words, into Palestinian territory, has now formally become an inaccessible military zone. This is obviously an illegal and completely arbitrary imposition. Please try to imagine what a kilometre-wide band means in a strip of land like Gaza, which is only six kilometres wide, or rather narrow, at certain points. Within those six kilometres live thousands of people, who wish to farm their land and simply provide themselves with something to eat. As if bullets against unarmed civilians weren't enough, the Israeli Army entertains itself with pyromania too. They cross the borders and set fields cultivated with wheat and barley on fire; these harvests are the sole source of sustenance for hundreds of families.

Early each morning in my portside flat, I wake up with a start at the sound of artillery fire from the Israeli Navy, preventing rudimentary Palestinian fishing boats from sailing further than three miles from the coast. This is yet another unilateral and illegal limit imposed by Israel as a form of collective punishment, breaking Article 33 of the Fourth Geneva Convention. In recent months, about 30 fishermen have been kidnapped and taken to Israel where their boats were confiscated. Since 18th January, 25 Palestinians were killed, many of them fishermen and farmers. In the same period, thankfully no additional victims have been recorded on the Israeli side, even with the occasional launch of a Qassam 'rocket'. Preventing farming and fishing, destroying irrigation systems, uprooting plants and destroying dozens and dozens of acres of crops, and, finally, firing on fishermen and farmers is all part of the systematic oppression of the Palestinian people. It's a constant stranglehold on the economy, which impoverishes the population until they're forced to live off humanitarian aid.

Occasionally, some youth reach a point where they've had enough of living without dignity under an inhuman siege, struggling to earn a living for themselves and their families. Perhaps the Israelis may have killed their fathers or brothers in the fields or at sea. So they'll enrol in some brigade, shoot some homemade rocket towards Israel, just to prove how heroic it is to fight for one's people, perhaps trying to convince themselves more than their enemy.

No Western government protests strongly against the genocidal siege that Gaza is forced to endure, yet for these randomly shot 'rockets', thankfully almost always shot without causing any harm, Europe and America's governments are ready to legitimize a massacre such as the last one endured in Gaza. We all know too well, as is also common knowledge in Tel Aviv, that if Palestinian farmers and fishermen were allowed to live and work exactly as their Israeli counterparts, almost no one here would be tempted to shoot Qassam 'rockets' against Sderot or Ashkelon. But the Israeli Army continues to ensure that the cost of merely living and working in Gaza must remain very steep. The change so often evoked with President Barack Obama's inauguration has not really taken place. No one in the new US administration has even deigned to visit Gaza so far. You cannot change the situation in the Middle East if you're not willing to really familiarize yourself with it and understand it fully. This negligence literally robs me of sleep.

John Kennedy once gave a famous speech in West Berlin 1963. Kennedy said, 'Two thousand years ago the proudest boast was "civis Romanus sum". Today, in the world of freedom, the proudest boast is "Ich bin ein Berliner".' He added that,

> There are many people in the world who really don't understand, or say they don't, what is the great issue between the free world and the Communist world. Let them come to Berlin. There are some who say that Communism is the wave of the future. Let them come to Berlin. And there are some who say in Europe and elsewhere we can work with the Communists. Let them come to Berlin. And there are even a few who say that it is true that Communism is an evil system, but it permits us to make economic progress. *Lass' sie nach Berlin kommen.* Let them come to Berlin.

As suggested by Italian blogger, Milena Spigaglia, paraphrasing Kennedy that speech could be rewritten thus to address the siege of Gaza today:

> There are many people in the world that cannot understand, or claim they don't understand what the deal between Palestine and Israel is. Let them come to Gaza. Some say that Israel is the force of the future. Let them come to Gaza. Others claim, in Europe and elsewhere, that we are able to cooperate with the Israelis. Let them come to Gaza. And there are even some who say that it's true, Israel is evil, but it allows for economic progress. Let them come to Gaza.

Underneath the layers of destruction and rubble, Gaza shines like an icon and, at the same time, stands as a mark of shame. For those, like myself, who've shared the trials of its inhabitants so intimately, to the point of becoming a fellow citizen and, subsequently, a prisoner with no way out, Gaza is the symbol of persistent resistance against titanic oppression. David's little slingshot hangs off Ahmed's belt against a Hebrew-speaking Goliath, who brandishes his DIME and white phosphorous. Gaza is a metaphor for a humanity that doesn't want to be eclipsed in the silence and shame of those who've already resigned themselves to extinction. Gaza is not yet entirely a land of crumbling tombstones, but is still filled with human beings with hearts like mountains whose inscrutable gaze looks towards an uncertain future.

Stay human.

Timeline

1948-9 Al-Naka/Israeli war of independence
Boundaries of Gaza Strip set
Gaza put under Egyptian administration

1964 Establishment of the PLO

1967 Six Day War
Gaza occupied by Israeli forces

1969 Yasser Arafat become Chairman of the PLO

1987 Establishment of Hamas
First Intifada begins

1993 End of First Intifada

1994 Palestinian Authority takes administrative
control of the Gaza Strip under Oslo Accords
Construction of land barrier between Israel
and Gaza begins

2000 Second Intifada begins

2004 Assassinations of Hamas leaders, Ahmed
Yassin and Abdel Aziz al-Rantisi
Death of Yasser Arafat

2005	Israel removes settlers from the Gaza Strip but maintains border controls
2006	Hamas wins over half the seats in the Palestinian parliamentary elections
	Conflict between Israel and Gaza
2007	Palestinian civil conflict between Hamas and Fatah
	Fatah takes control of the West Bank, Hamas controls the Gaza Strip
	Palestinian Authority declares state of emergency
	Israel declares Gaza a 'hostile entity'
	Gaza's borders closed and Israel's economic blockade of Gaza begins
2008	Intensification of conflict between Israel and Gaza
	27th December: Attack on Gaza by Israel led by air-strikes
	29th December: Air-strikes on the University of Gaza; attack on the *Dignity*
2009	3rd January: Israeli ground troops enter Gaza
	6th January: Bombing of an UNRWA school
	18th January: Unilateral ceasefire declared by Israel
	21st January: Israel claims complete troop withdrawal
	5th November: UN General Assembly votes that Israel and Hamas be referred to International Criminal Court for war crimes

Background Notes

Gaza

Forty kilometres long and 10 kilometres wide, with a population of over 1.5 million inhabitants, the Gaza Strip is one of the most densely populated areas in the world. Its boundaries were fixed after the Israeli-Arab conflict of 1948-9. Under an Egyptian administration for the following 19 years, the Strip was occupied by Israel in 1967, at the end of the Six Day War. After the Oslo Accords, it came under the partial administrative control of the Palestinian Authority in 1994. While Israel unilaterally withdrew its settlements in 2005, she retained control of Gaza's land and sea borders, along with Egypt. Gaza's land borders are surrounded by a barrier, constructed by Israel between 1994 and 2004, separating it from Israel and Egypt. There are three main passes: Erez in the north, serving as a passageway to and from Israel; Karni in the east, used for the transit of trucks; and Rafah in the south, connecting it with Egypt.

UNRWA

After the end of the first Israeli-Arab conflict, with Resolution 302 of 8th December 1949, the United Nations founded UNRWA, an Agency assisting the 4.6 million Palestinian refugees in the Middle East. Among these,

478,272 live in eight refugee camps: Jabalia, Rafah, Shati, Nuseirat, Khan Yunis, Bureij, Maghazi and Deir el-Balah. The camps are overcrowded. In the Shati camp over 80,000 people – the equivalent of the entire Palestinian population in Gaza before the Nakba – live in an area measuring one square kilometre. Since its establishment, UNRWA has managed to set up 187 schools, 18 surgeries, and supports 86,971 refugees who are classified as being in 'extreme need'.

Al-Nakba

The first Israeli-Arab war took place between 1948 and 1949. For Israel, it would come to be known as a 'war of independence' and for the Palestinians as 'Al-Nakba', or 'The Catastrophe'. Between 650,000 and 800,000 Palestinians were driven from their homes and became refugees. Academics are split on the reasons of this flight, but 'new historians' in Israel agree on the fact that – at least in part – it was due to proven operations of ethnic cleansing carried out by Jewish militias.

PLO

The PLO (Munazzamat al-Tahrir al-Filastiniyyat or the Palestinian Liberation Organization) is a political and paramilitary organisation established in 1964. It is recognised by over 100 states, including Israel since 1993, as the sole and legitimate representative of the Palestinian people. It is coalition of largely secular Palestinian groups committed to the national liberation of the Palestinians, the largest faction being Fatah, which is left-wing and nationalist in orientation. It came to prominence after the Six Day War of 1967,

and led a long guerrilla war against Israel from the 1960s
until entering into peace negotiations in the 1990s. Histori-
cally, it was dominated by the leadership of Yasser Arafat
from 1969 until his death in 2004.

First Intifada

An uprising between 1987 and 1993 against Israeli rule
in the Palestinian Territories, which began in the refugee
camp of Jabalia and spread to the rest of Gaza, East
Jerusalem and the West Bank. The Intifada consisted of acts
of civil disobedience like strikes, boycotts of Israeli goods,
barricading, refusal to pay taxes and demonstrations that
included stone-throwing by youths, as well as violence
directed as Israeli soldiers and civilians alike. Over 1000
Palestinians were killed by Israeli forces and 160 Israelis
were killed by Palestinians; about a thousand Palestinians
were killed in internal strife.

Hamas

Hamas (Harakat al-Muqawama al-Islamiyya or the 'Islamic
Resistance Movement) was established in Gaza in 1987,
formed at the beginning of the first Intifada, and has
its roots in the Palestinian wing of the Egyptian Muslim
Brotherhood. Its short term-goal is to drive Israeli forces
out of the Palestinian Occupied Territories. Its long-term
goal, as stated in its Charter, is to establish an Islamic state
in all of historic Palestine, which includes the state of
Israel. For years, its activities have included social works
like building schools, hospitals and religious institutions,
and military operations carried out by its affiliated militia,
the Izz Al-Din Al-Qassam Brigades. Since 2006, Hamas

has emerged as a major rival to the PLO and Fatah since achieving victory in the Palestinian Authority legislative elections, particularly in Gaza.

Second Intifada

The second Intifada, also known as the Al-Aqsa Intifada, began in September 2000 and has included, like the first Intifada, civil disobedience and paramilitary action. Up until April 2008, it has been estimated that 5,500 Palestinians and over 1,000 Israelis have been killed; in the same period, over 550 Palestinians were killed in internal strife.

Disengagement from Gaza

In the summer of 2005, the Israeli Army acted a plan that had been announced by Prime Minister Ariel Sharon a year earlier. Settlers and troops were withdrawn from the Strip. The plan had been initially dubbed the 'tokhnit hahafrada' or 'separation plan' by Sharon, but was renamed as the 'disengagement plan' so as not to evoke memories of South African apartheid. Between 17th August and 12th September, about 8,000 settlers occupying 21 settlements were evacuated. Hamas's propaganda boasted the Israeli withdrawal as a 'victory of the resistance'. In an interview, Dov Weissglass – then Director of the Prime Minister's Office – remarked that: 'The disengagement is actually formaldehyde. It supplies the amount of formaldehyde that's necessary so that there will not be a political process with the Palestinians.'[15]

---

15. Ari Shavit, 'The Big Freeze', *Haaretz*, 8th October 2004.

But it wasn't the end of the occupation

And according to Tel Aviv, from the moment that Israel had withdrawn its troops and settlers, it no longer occupied Gaza, and therefore no longer had direct responsibility for its inhabitants. However, according to international law, matters don't quite work this way. All border passes (excluding Rafah), not to mention Gaza's airspace and maritime borders, remain under Israeli control, and therefore freedom of movement and trade are externally controlled. The disengagement plan states that 'Israel will hold sole control of Gaza airspace and will continue to carry out military activity in the waters of the Gaza Strip.'

Qassam Rockets

From the start of the Second Intifada, Gaza's militants started shooting Qassam rockets at nearby Israeli towns: Sderot, for example, being just a kilometre away from the Strip. Made in Gaza, these are simple two-metre long metal tubes that filled with homemade explosives. While they are easy to transport from one launch site to the next, their trajectory cannot be guided, and they have a range of between three and 10 kilometres. During Operation 'Cast Lead', some Russian-made Grad ('Katyusha') rockets were also shot. About 15 Israelis have so far been killed by these rudimentary rockets.

Targeted Assassinations

Israel has long adopted a policy of targeted assassination against those deemed to represent 'a threat to the security' of Israel. With the Second Intifada, however, reliance on this tactic – deploying the air force and the mistaravim (elite units disguised as Arabs) – has been on the increase. Among the most notable targets were the co-founders of Hamas, Sheikh Ahmed Yassin and Abdel Aziz al-Rantisi, who were both killed in 2004. According to human rights organizations, dozens of civilians were killed during these not-so-precise targeted assassinations, which were condemned by the EU and discribed by the US as 'not being an aid to peace'. On 23rd July 2002, the Israeli Air Force dropped a one-tonne bomb on a building in Gaza, not only killing the head of the Izz al-Din Qassim Brigades, Salah Shehade, but a further 15 people, including nine children.

Hamas wins the elections

George Bush's US administration often employed the rhetoric of 'democratic reform' as a central part of its strategy for the Middle East. At the same time, the magical formula for the Palestinians was free elections. On 25th January 2006, Hamas achieved a landslide victory, earning 74 seats in the Palestinian parliament against the 45 gained by Fatah. It's a 'revolution' that turns the political picture on its head. In previous elections a decade earlier, Fatah had won 68 out of 88 seats. Hamas's victory sparks a conflict between the two parties.

Fatah-Hamas Conflict

In June 2007, following months of mutual accusations, armed clashes and feuds, Hamas's militia chases Fatah's political leadership and its militias, led by Mohammed Dahlan, out of the Gaza Strip. Dahlan was accused by Hamas of corruption and of being at the beck and call of the US and Israel. On 14th June, 2007, the President of the Palestinian National Authority, Mahmoud Abbas, dissolved the unity government, and dismissed Ismail Haniyeh (Hamas), one of the PNA's two Prime Ministers. Subsequently, Fatah gained control of the occupied West Bank.

Israel loses no time

Compared with 2005, the Israeli government reduces by a quarter the basic goods and supplies destined for the Gaza Strip. Only humanitarian aid filters through, while a complete ban of exports paralyzes the Palestinian economy. The Israeli authorities then arrested dozens of Hamas deputies. After the launch of homemade Qassam rockets on 19th September 2007, the Israeli government branded the Gaza Strip a 'hostile entity'. The UN Secretary General, Ban Ki-Moon, then warned that this clashed with Israel's obligations under international humanitarian law towards the civilian population of Gaza.

Targeting Hundreds of Civilians

The figures provided by the Israel Security Agency ('Shin Bet') in January 2008 shed a sinister light on what happens in Gaza. In the years 2006-7, 810 people were killed in the Strip, among whom were 200 that were 'clearly not linked to terrorist organizations'. The newspaper *Haaretz*, however, counted 360 civilians among 816 dead. B'Tselem, the Israeli human rights organisation, reported that 152 casualties were younger than 18 and 48 were younger than 14. The Home Security Minister, Avi Dichter, announced that 5% of the Strip's militants have been killed', adding that the number of militants were estimated at around

20,000. But if reported rates of civilian deaths are taken into account, then this would entail that the elimination of remaining 'combatants' by the Israeli Army and Air Force would also mean murdering a further 8,823 civilians along with them.

Massacre

To put an end, officially, to the launch of Qassam rockets, one of which had killed a student, Roni Yechiah, at Sapir College in Sderot, on 27th February 2008, the Israeli Army and Air Force launched a draconian attack on the Gaza Strip, killing 120 Palestinians. Half of these, according to B'Tselem, are not fighters. While the massacre unfolds, Deputy Defence Minister Matan Vilnai threatened a 'shoah' (holocaust) against the Gaza Strip.

One out of three is unemployed

According to a World Bank report published on 27th April 2008, the unemployment rate in Gaza stood at 33% (23% in the West Bank). It is predicted that this will rise because of layoffs in industry. Furthermore, 35% of the population lives in great poverty, and, without external aid in the form of food supplies and remittances from Palestinians abroad, it would rise to 67%. The World Bank report judges that Israeli restrictions are the main cause of the Strip's economic deterioration. In order to survive the embargo, Gazans built dozens of tunnels connecting Rafah to Egypt through which food, medicine, and merchandise of every sort, as well as weapons, are smuggled in. The tunnels are also used to smuggle those needing vital medical treatment into Egypt.

Operation 'Cast Lead'

Operation 'Cast Lead' started on 27th December 2008. During the three-week military operation, 1,285 Palestinians were killed. According to the data collected by the Palestinian Center for Human Rights, an authoritative and independent NGO, 895 are civilians and 167 are policemen. There are 280 slaughtered children and 111 women among the dead. The injured total 4,336 (including 1,133 children and 735 women). Some 2,400 houses were entirely destroyed by the army and the air force, in addition to 28 public buildings, 30 mosques and 121 shops. On 18th January 2009, just two days before US President Barack Obama's inauguration, Israel announced a unilateral ceasefire and started pulling its troops out of Gaza, concluding the operation three days later. 'Changing the reality' of Gaza and 'hitting hard against Hamas' had been the slogans of Tel Aviv's government to justify the offensive. Yet the attack has strengthened rather than lessened Hamas's authority in the Gaza Strip.

War crimes done with impunity

Dozens of human rights organizations have started collecting evidence of 'war crimes', incriminating Israeli military leaders and politicians who planned and executed Operation 'Cast Lead'. At the time of writing, the track of future legal action is unclear, although an opportunity exists in a few countries like Great Britain which allows for the prosecution of foreign citizens for 'crimes against humanity' and 'genocide'. The longer and more difficult legal path would be to take Israel to the International Criminal Court in The Hague for war crimes, although

Israel, like the US, does not recognise the ICC. In November 2009, the UN General Assembly called for the UN Goldstone Report (which alleged there had been grave breaches of the Geneva Conventions, involving 'individual criminal responsibility', in the case of the Gaza War of 2008-9) should be referred to the ICC.